making

room

for

god

"Mary Sperry shows us how to place our physical and mental clutter into the context of our spiritual lives as followers of Christ. More than a how-to book, *Making Room for God* offers Sperry's expertise on scripture and the teachings of the Church as organic elements of her writing. Her purpose is to not only save us money and time but also save our souls. By sharing her own journey with wit and humility, Sperry becomes our companion for a process that can be overwhelming yet rewarding because it's life-changing. This book will revolutionize your life. Let it help you take your stewardship of God's gifts seriously. I really love this book!"

Lisa M. Hendey
Founder of *CatholicMom.com* and author of *The Grace of Yes*

"Mary Sperry's purifying confessions and practical suggestions about what we can do to make room for God and others by decluttering should be required reading for every Christian seeking to make the world a better place. Too much stuff is a spiritual problem that Sperry's wisdom can help us deal with, manage, and in the end, overcome."

Sr. Rose Pacatte, F.S.P.
Author of *Martin Sheen: Pilgrim on the Way*

"With wit, wisdom, and warmth, Mary Sperry offers us some of the best practical and spiritual advice on how to clear out the clutter of our closets—and our lives."

Deacon Greg Kandra
Blogger and journalist at *Aleteia*

"*Making Room for God* is a spiritual challenge that will lead you to holier, healthier habits for relating to your possessions, to an interior conversion, and to a deeper relationship with God."

Michele Faehnle and **Emily Jaminet**
Authors of *Divine Mercy for Moms*

"In *Making Room for God*, Mary Sperry offers something most of us desperately need by expertly walking us through the practical side of decluttering and simplifying our lives. But she does so much more than demonstrate how to organize our sock drawers and kitchen cabinets. By acknowledging that the spiritual touches each part of our lives, no matter how small, Sperry guides the reader through an examination of the heart. While our worldly goods may be a mess, it's our souls that need the real spring cleaning, and this little book is ready to guide you through each step."

Haley Stewart
Catholic writer, speaker, podcaster, and blogger at *Carrots for Michaelmas*

making

room

for

god

decluttering and the spiritual life

Mary Elizabeth Sperry

Ave Maria Press AVE Notre Dame, Indiana

Founded in 1865, Ave Maria Press is a ministry of the United States Province of Holy Cross.

www.avemariapress.com

Paperback: ISBN-13 978-1-59471-797-0

E-book: ISBN-13 978-1-59471-798-7

Cover image © www.gettyimages.com.

Cover and text design by Katherine Robinson.

Printed and bound in the United States of America.

Library of Congress Cataloging-in-Publication Data

Names: Sperry, Mary Elizabeth, author.
Title: Making room for God : decluttering and the spiritual life / Mary Elizabeth Sperry.
Description: Notre Dame : Ave Maria Press, 2018.
Identifiers: LCCN 2017043761 (print) | LCCN 2017052444 (ebook) | ISBN 9781594717987 (ebook) | ISBN 9781594717970 (pbk.)
Subjects: LCSH: Spiritual life--Catholic Church. | Simplicity--Religious aspects--Catholic Church.
Classification: LCC BX2350.3 (ebook) | LCC BX2350.3 .S646 2018 (print) | DDC
    248.4 / 82--dc23
LC record available at https://lccn.loc.gov/2017043761

For Christopher, with love

Contents

Preface

My name is Mary, and I'm a pack rat. That's bad enough. But to make it worse, I'm also cheap. Now, some of my friends try to fancy that up and say I'm frugal, but I know the truth. I'm cheap. I hate to throw anything away if it has even a little bit of useful life left. I got a brand new wallet for Christmas a few years ago. I don't use it. After all, my old wallet is still perfectly good. Okay, so the zipper pulls have fallen off and I need to use my fingernails to open it. But it's still good, right? Why use something new when the old one is fine? And it's not like I could even donate the old wallet. Who besides me would want it?

The never throwing anything out wouldn't be so bad if I had a huge house. However, I live in 847 square feet. It's not quite as small as a "tiny house," but it sure seems like it at times. Especially when it's shared with an eight-pound rescue terrier who has a raft of toys she never plays with and an entire wardrobe of T-shirts and sweaters.

While my situation may not seem all that strange to you (well, except for the doggie wardrobe thing), it really is quite unusual. For most of human history, life was a daily battle against scarcity. People struggled to survive harsh climates and make do without enough food or fresh water, and with limited space and privacy, minimal furniture and household goods, and only a few changes of clothing. Even fifty years ago, a child having his or her own room, let alone one filled with clothes, toys, books, and electronic gadgets, was a privilege reserved to a few.

Today, scarcity is still all too common for much of the world's population. Famine and drought can limit the availability of food and fresh water. Millions of people lack stable homes, living in foreign lands as refugees or traveling unceasingly as migrants, fleeing crime, warfare, and crushing poverty. They are often forced to leave with nothing more than the clothes on their backs and whatever else they can carry. Each day is marked by fear and the difficult decisions necessary when too little is shared among too many.

But for many people in the developed world, the problem is completely reversed. They, or should I say *we*, struggle to deal with challenges caused by having too much. My house, and maybe yours, is filled with clutter. Making dinner requires digging through multiple cabinets and drawers to find a misplaced utensil. (I didn't make mashed potatoes for two months because I couldn't find my potato masher.) Too many clothes stuff our drawers and closets, yet we can find nothing to wear. Mountains of paperwork cover tables (and floors!) and fill file cabinets, making it take hours to find an important receipt or letter. And let's not even start on the attic, basement, or garage—where clutter lives in retirement. As I write this, an entire corner of my attic is filled with the empty boxes from appliances I no longer own. That's right, the appliances have gone to the great beyond, but the boxes remain an attractive housing option for the squirrels that decide to winter in my attic.

And clutter is not limited to papers and things. Our computers are full of mystery files and uncategorized photos. (I still have floppy disks! I don't have a computer that can read them, but I still have the disks.) E-mail inboxes are filled with spam and ads, so we miss the messages we actually want. I almost lost a job opportunity because the offer got mixed in with the spam. Our calendars are cluttered with too much to do and not enough time. Even our minds are cluttered with more thoughts than we can manage.

"Storage solutions" have become big business. Rental of storage units is a bigger business (in dollars) than the Hollywood movie business. Once used for furniture and other household goods between moves or during extended travel, storage units have become the go-to resting place for holiday decorations, unused (and sometimes broken!) appliances, books, memorabilia, and other random items. (I still have stuff in my mom's storage unit. If you offered me a million dollars to tell you ten things I have stored there, you'd take your money home.) Storage facilities advertise their ease of access, safety, and even climate control. Yes, in many cases, our junk enjoys better living conditions than much of the world's human population.

Not surprisingly, the organizing and decluttering industry has grown by leaps and bounds as well. Everyone from specialty retailers to big-box stores market ways to organize and shelve our belongings. We can find a company to build a custom closet with a dedicated place for every item of clothing and accessory. I see ads in magazines with organized storage areas looking absolutely perfect, and my heart starts to beat a little faster—and then I realize that some of these closets are bigger than my guest room! We can hire a personal coach to help us deal with our clutter or downsize to a smaller home. Type *declutter* into a search engine and you'll unearth more than two million results, including books, magazine articles, television shows, and blogs, offering hints and strategies for decluttering. Ironically, the decluttering industry is itself quite cluttered. And recently, it has spawned a new, more radical dimension: minimalism. Individuals choosing this lifestyle have chosen to intentionally withdraw from the culture of consumption and to buy and own as little as possible. This freedom from things gives them the freedom to use their time and money in other ways. Minimalists have produced a variety of blogs and books to explain their philosophy and to offer advice on paring back possessions.

So what makes *this* book different? This book isn't just about the state of your house; it's about the state of your soul. As I continue to wage battle against the clutter in my house, I've discovered that clutter not only has practical and financial implications; it has spiritual consequences as well. Now I can hear you smirking and eye-rolling: "Does she really expect me to believe that God cares about the mess in my file cabinet? And that the stuff in my closet has something to do with my spiritual life? Seriously?" Well, yes, I do. Because, you see, the fundamental claim of Christianity is quite simple. God loves us so much that he sent his Son to us as a human being—to live and die, to work and sleep, to make or purchase clothing and eat meals—just like we do. And because of God's gracious and abiding love, nothing we do, no matter how mundane or unspiritual it seems, is beneath God's notice: "Are not five sparrows sold for two small coins? Yet not one of them has escaped the notice of God. Even the hairs of your head have all been counted. Do not be afraid. You are worth more than many sparrows" (Lk 12:6–7).

Some early Church Fathers and Mothers fled into the desert to get away from the influences of the Roman Empire, to face their own spiritual demons, and to draw closer to God. They lived alone in small cells, wearing little more than rags, owning nothing, and eating as little as possible. In many ways, they were the spiritual forebears of today's minimalists. The desert fathers and mothers gave up every worldly comfort so that they would have the freedom to love God unreservedly. Now, I'm not going to that extreme. I'm not going to abandon my house and job to live alone on a mountainside (although there are times when that sounds appealing). However, I am learning that dealing with clutter can help me to deal with some of the barriers that keep me from living as the person God calls me to be.

Each chapter in this book will follow the same pattern. First, I'll share a bit of my spiritual journey, especially the spiritual realities I've struggled to understand as I've tried to reduce the clutter in my house and make sure that it doesn't come back. I will look at my own decluttering efforts with the eyes of faith, trying to live the spiritual values I hold dear. When possible, I will share some of the guidance I've drawn from Church teaching and from the example and advice of the holy women and men who have gone before us. Then, I will describe my efforts at decluttering in more detail. Perhaps my experience will give you some ideas to help with your own decluttering. It will either make you feel better about your own situation or let you know that you are not alone in the struggle. Finally, I'll offer some next steps to help guide your own efforts. But since this book isn't just about decluttering, I'll also offer some questions for reflection. You may want to pray about these questions or write about them in a journal. If you are reading this book with friends, you may want to discuss them as a group.

One caution before we dig any further into the problem of clutter. The sort of clutter I'm talking about here is very different than what mental health specialists classify as hoarding disorder. People who struggle with hoarding continue to accumulate possessions even when they have no more room and the possessions themselves have no value. For example, someone might collect hundreds of straws or sugar packets from a fast food restaurant. Hoarders have a great deal of difficulty discarding any possessions. In the most serious cases, some people will not even discard trash. Some hoarders may invest their identity in their possessions so that any suggestion about discarding some things is seen as a personal attack. Finally, hoarding can inhibit the ordinary activities of life. For example, a person may not be able to cook dinner because his oven is stuffed with old magazines. Hoarding can threaten health and safety. It should be addressed with professional help.

Every journey worth taking starts from, and leads to, God. It's time now to begin this one.

1.

Why Declutter?

Let's start our look at the practical side of decluttering by addressing a simple but profound question: Why? What does decluttering get me that I value?

Decluttering Saves Time

Time is my most valuable resource. No matter how hard I try, I can't make more time. I can only change how I use the time I have. As I get older, time seems to move even faster and each minute feels that much more precious. Yet every minute seems to have more claims on it. There are so many things I *have* to do that it seems impossible to find time to do the things I *want* to do, such as read a good book, or even find time for the things I *should* do, such as pray more or volunteer in the community. So how does decluttering save time?

First, a home with less clutter is easier to keep clean. Clutter attracts more clutter, and all clutter attracts dust. Picking up dozens of things to dust them takes forever, so I tend not to do it until it's absolutely necessary—and then it takes even longer. Moving piles of things so that I can use the dining room table or vacuum the living room floor can more than double the time it takes to complete a simple chore. Even putting away clean laundry in already stuffed drawers and closets takes longer.

Second, decluttering makes it far more likely that I can find things when I need them. If I added up all the minutes I've spent looking for utensils or storage containers in my disorganized kitchen cabinets, I'd have time for a vacation! Let's face it; having to take everything out of the shed to find the hedge clippers is just a waste of time. How many hours have you spent looking for a bill or an invitation that disappeared into a stack of unfiled papers? How often do your kids have to upend their backpacks to find the form that has to be signed and returned tomorrow?

Deciding to declutter can help you use time more efficiently. An organized closet can make getting ready in the morning much faster. If your closet is organized and decluttered, it's easy to see your wardrobe options and less likely that the clothes you choose will come out a crumpled mess, requiring ironing or a trip to the dry cleaner. (I have clothes that I almost never wear not because I don't like them or they don't fit but because they require ironing and I rarely have time in the morning to break out the ironing board.) A decluttered home makes it less likely that you will misplace or forget something important. Imagine—no more lost receipts or last-minute runs to the school to deliver forgotten lunches!

Decluttering Saves Money

Decluttering saves money by reducing purchases. You begin to scrutinize your purchases more carefully, trying to avoid buying anything unnecessary. You avoid new purchases by using up all the things you had forgotten that you owned but that decluttering unearthed. During a recent decluttering of my bathroom cabinet, I found enough shampoo, soap, dental floss, and toothpaste to meet my needs for almost a year! (To be honest, I found so much dental floss that I gave it to a friend who is a nun. Now all the sisters in her convent have clean teeth!) Cleaning out a closet allowed me to find lovely handmade items purchased on long-ago trips. Many of these items make great gifts, meaning I don't need to buy other gifts. Decluttering my bedroom closet and dresser drawers led to finding great outfits that I'd forgotten I owned. I hadn't worn these clothes in so long it was like I bought a whole new wardrobe without spending a cent.

A decluttered house makes you far less likely to purchase a duplicate of something you already have. You know how the cycle goes. You buy a birthday card for your mom and forget where you put it, so you have to buy another. You end up with a stack of unused (and sometimes crushed and unusable) cards. I could fill this book with examples from my life, and you could probably do the same.

Lack of clutter saves money by making it less likely that you will lose things, incurring late fees and fines. Recent surveys indicate that almost a quarter of adults have paid a bill late not because they didn't have the money but because they couldn't find the bill! Three years ago, I had to go to Rome for a business meeting. As you might imagine, I was really excited—until I couldn't find my passport. I spent weeks in an increasingly frantic search, looking every place I thought it might be. With my trip less than six weeks away, I gave up and decided to declare it lost and get a new one. The trip to my hometown to get a copy of my birth certificate, the extra fee for expedited handling, and the regular renewal fee I was paying five years early means that little mistake cost me two vacation days and about $300. I finally found the old passport eighteen months later. It was buried in a bunch of old papers I'd tossed in a box to get them out of the way.

Decluttering Reduces Stress

Scarcity causes a stress response. When you need something that you don't have, your mind and body respond with a more rapid heartbeat, faster and shallower breathing, agitated movements, a quicker temper, less patience, and even mild panic. It's hard to remain calm and kind when you have to get out the door to catch your plane and you can't remember where you put your keys.

Even beyond these crisis situations, a space that is less cluttered and more organized is calming to the eye and the spirit. Decluttered spaces invite you to sit, rest, read, and spend time with the people you love. It's calming to know where things are when you need them. Getting rid of the clutter can remove dozens of little stressors that disrupt your days and disturb your peace.

Decluttering Opens New Possibilities

A surprising number of people never invite friends and neighbors into their homes because of clutter. They are embarrassed that their houses aren't tidy, so they are unwilling to open their doors. There's nowhere to sit. The dining room table is covered with paperwork and half-finished craft projects. Inviting guests into the clutter seems to cause more trouble than it's worth. Furthermore, the "lifestyle" industry has brainwashed us to believe that we shouldn't entertain unless we have a home ready to be photographed for a magazine spread, with perfectly clean spaces accented with perfectly matched, fashionable accessories, and a multi-course gourmet meal served on heirloom china. In the real world, most people we call friends will happily overlook some clutter and will be more than content with a simple meal and some pleasant conversation. Still, fear and clutter keep us from extending the invitation. Or you may be like me and invite people anyway—and then spend half the evening apologizing for the clutter and mess.

How often have you begun a sentence with some form of the phrase, "Once I get the house in order/the filing done/this project finished, I can . . ."? Whatever finishes that sentence is an opportunity that clutter has stolen from you. When anything keeps you from embracing opportunities filled with meaning and joy, that thing becomes a prison. I often feel that clutter has become a prison of my own making. I have the keys. It's time to open the door and step out into new freedom.

Thoughts for the Journey

- How does clutter affect my daily life and my relationships? Are these effects positive or negative?
- Why do I want to declutter? What do I hope to get from my efforts?

2.

Memories and Materialism

I start with the best of intentions. Really, I do. I decide that it's time to do some serious tidying—maybe clear off the top of the dresser so that I can actually use the mirror. I start going through the stuff I've just tossed there, throwing some things away and sorting other items so I can put them where they belong. And that's where the trouble starts. Putting toiletries away in the bathroom cabinet is impossible because it's too crowded. The papers I discover don't fit in the files. And there's no room in the desk for the office supplies. (And why were there paper clips on my dresser anyway?) Starting to declutter just shows me how much I really need to do to make my house tidy. Every time I look at the seemingly unending mountain of things to sort and organize, the word "blowtorch" comes to mind. It has to be easier to just toss everything and start over again with as little as possible.

God's Path
God Saw That It Was Good

Even beginning to think about decluttering can be over-whelming. During particularly stressful times, I'll binge on those blogs about minimalism and stare for hours at photos of cleverly designed "tiny houses." Even though these houses usually have fewer than five hundred square feet, everything has its place, the space is open and tidy, and it's always ready for guests to drop in. Then I think about how much I'd have to clear out of the living room to find a place for a friend to sit if she stopped by. Having someone stay overnight can require weeks of planning to unearth the bed in the guest room. It's got to be under the stacks of filing and craft supplies, right? I see articles about people who carry all of their worldly possessions in a single suitcase and I realize that I carry more than that to work each day.

There's certainly nothing wrong with making a conscious decision to limit our possessions. Religious women and men, and all who follow the evangelical counsel of poverty, choose to refrain from ownership of goods. Even their personal items, such as clothes and shoes, are owned by the community and only loaned to the members. People embrace evangelical poverty to avoid every tie that might limit their ability to love God and others freely and wholeheartedly.

But the spiritual value of poverty doesn't mean that material things are bad. In fact, if material things are bad, there's no great merit in avoiding them. If we seek to live holy and virtuous lives, avoiding bad things is the basic first step.

The book of Genesis, the very first pages of the Bible, reminds us time and again of the goodness of creation. As

God creates each element of the material world, scripture records the same refrain: "God saw that it was good."

But you don't have to take my word for it. From the earliest days of the Church, Christians maintained that people who held to the belief that the created world was bad and that only things of the spirit could be good were not speaking the truth. Some of these people even went so far as to claim that the God who created the world was not the same God revealed by Jesus Christ as his Father. The Church rejected this dualist understanding (things are bad; spirit is good) and consistently professed its belief in the goodness of the created world. Even more, the Church has maintained that creation itself bears witness to God (see *Catechism of the Catholic Church*, 32). This belief echoes the words of the psalmist: "The heavens declare the glory of God;/the firmament proclaims the works of his hands" (Ps 19:2).

St. Augustine, one of the great thinkers of the early Church, wrote a beautiful poem maintaining that creation itself reveals God's truth. We find it in volume 3 of the *Liturgy of the Hours*:

> "The Beauty of Creation Bears Witness to God"
> Question the beauty of the earth,
> the beauty of the sea,
> the beauty of the wide air around you,
> the beauty of the sky;
> question the order of the stars,
> the sun whose brightness lights the day,
> the moon whose splendor softens the gloom of night;
> question the living creatures that move in the waters,
> that roam upon the earth,
> that fly through the air;

the spirit that lies hidden,
the matter that is manifest;
the visible things that are ruled,
the invisible that rule them;
question all these.
They will answer you:
"Behold and see, we are beautiful."
Their beauty is their confession of God.
Who made these beautiful changing things,
if not one who is beautiful and changeth not.

In the late nineteenth century, Jesuit poet Gerard Manley Hopkins used his art to express the relationship between God and his creation, saying, "The world is charged with the grandeur of God."

Fighting Forgetfulness

So do the things I own bring me closer to God or push me further away? Can the things surrounding me help me see the hand of God in my life?

I've been involved in "church things" since I was a little girl. I remember paging through a picture Bible before I could read, either making up stories to go along with the pictures or retelling myself stories that grown-ups had told me. I loved going to church. When I was in grade school, Benediction was one of my favorite things. I loved it, mostly because of the beautiful gold monstrance used to expose the Blessed Sacrament and the abundant use of fancy incense (which always made me cough). By the time I got to high school, I was volunteering as a sacristan in the high school chapel, learning how to iron purificators and corporals (cloths used at the altar) and keeping the vestments and vessels, as well as the chapel itself, in good order.

By the time I finished high school, my love for the Bible and for the Church's liturgy was entrenched so deeply that it was there to stay. I love the Bible because it's the story of real people trying to figure out how to love God and other people. I love liturgy because it uses the real things of this world to help us know God and his grace. In college, I was asked to serve as an Extraordinary Minister of the Eucharist. One year, the head chaplain asked if I could help distribute ashes on Ash Wednesday since I only had afternoon classes that day. (Okay, I *may* have cut statistics. Don't tell Father Joe.) At two consecutive services, I dipped my thumb into the ashes and smeared them on my classmates' foreheads, reminding them to "Repent and believe in the Gospel." By the end of the morning, the words were drilled into my brain and the ashes were embedded so deeply in my thumb that washing—even scrubbing—couldn't get them out. I had to wait for them to work their way out. For days, all I had to do was look at my right thumb to remember that I was ashes and dust. It was one of the best Lents of my life.

The Church keeps giving us these reminders—even daily! Through the sacraments, the Church continues to express the goodness of creation and the way it bears witness to God's goodness. We pour abundant water in the Sacrament of Baptism, and we anoint the baptized, the confirmed, and the ordained with sweet-smelling oil. We even anoint the sick with oil to soothe, strengthen, and heal. In celebrating the central mystery of our faith, the Eucharist, we use bread and wine—"the work of human hands." This simple food and drink, through the power of the Holy Spirit, become the very essence—the Body and Blood—of Christ. The seven sacraments instituted by

Christ are privileged ways that God shares his grace with us. They also serve as constant reminders that the things created by God are good and that God uses them to reveal his truth and to transmit his grace.

The Eucharist is a memorial. In the Mass, we remember Jesus' Passion, Death, and Resurrection—the loving, self-giving act that destroyed death and gives us the hope of eternal life. Part of the Eucharistic Prayer, the central prayer of the Mass, recounts God's action in Christ. The theological name for this part of the plan is *anamnesis*. You may recognize the root of the word *amnesia* in that term. Amnesia is a condition marked by memory loss—forgetting. This part of the Eucharistic Prayer is, quite literally, called the "not forgetting." We remember all the good things that God has done for us—most especially sending us his only Son. In this remembering, the mystery becomes real and present in our time and place.

Remembering plays a similar role in the other parts of life, too. For example, I hold on to certain things because they are physical reminders of special people or events in my life. They call forth treasured memories. They help me remember and make past events present to me again. In the process of decluttering, I fear losing these precious memories.

Remember I said that I don't like to throw things out? That goes double for clothes. If I say a dress is twenty-five years old, it's not because I bought it in a vintage store. It's been in my closet that long. I had one dress that I carried with me when I moved cross-country—despite the fact that it didn't fit anymore. It was just so tied to wonderful memories of the things I'd done wearing it that I couldn't give it away. When I finally did decide to put it in the donation bag, I had to drop the bag off that day in order to resist the temptation to put that dress back in the closet.

Even today, as I face yet another decluttering of my closet, there's one dress that I know I'll put back in, even though I haven't worn it for more than ten years. I've owned it for more than thirty years. It's beautifully made—the quintessential little black dress. But that's not why I keep it. When I was in my senior year of college, I had a big interview preceded by a cocktail party. I had a suit for the interview, but with two weeks to go, I didn't have a dress for cocktails with the interview team. My mom and dad were going on a church-sponsored day trip to Atlantic City. Jokingly, my mom said that if she won anything, she'd use it to buy me a dress. She won, and she used all of her winnings to buy that dress. It's probably the most money she ever spent on a single item of clothing apart from her wedding gown—and she gave it to me. Every time I look at that dress, I remember her love and her generosity and I'm overwhelmed again. You know, I'll probably be buried in that dress, going to God wrapped in my mom's love and generosity.

Earlier this year, I was sorting through a huge bag of papers. In among the obvious junk (coupons that expired in 2009!), I found some treasures. A note written by a friend I haven't spoken to in years. The last Christmas card a friend sent me before he unexpectedly passed away. Photos I'd forgotten I'd taken. As I put those things in the "save" pile, memories of good times and great conversations flooded back.

Decluttering isn't simply a matter of tossing out our abundance and living with less. The process of decluttering requires reflecting on the memories—good and bad—carried by the things we possess. Decluttering isn't just about discarding possessions. It's about limiting our possessions to things that are either necessary or truly memorable. As a sculptor carves away the excess to reveal the art hidden within the stone, by decluttering we carve away the excess to reveal what we value.

Gifts of a Loving God

Having possessions, even lots of possessions, isn't bad in and of itself. It's our relationship with those possessions that matters. Do we own our possessions, or do they own us? When acquiring, maintaining, organizing, displaying, and protecting our possessions begins to take over our lives, keeping us from dedicating time to the activities we claim are our priorities, then possessions have become our masters. Decluttering can be a way to change the balance and reaffirm our priorities.

The proper relationship with possessions is described as stewardship. Most church members are acquainted with this term because of the annual parish stewardship appeal when we commit to how much we will donate to our parish in the coming year. That association can lead us to believe that stewardship is about donating more money to charity and committing more time to volunteer efforts. While those things are important, they do not encompass everything that stewardship is. Stewardship is a reset of our relationship with all creation, including our talents and our time. A proper understanding of stewardship begins with a simple realization: everything we are and everything we possess is the gift of a loving God. We respond to this gracious, unmerited gift with gratitude.

If we begin with gratitude, we won't hold on to things too tightly and we will need to acquire less. Gratitude and stewardship make our possessions reminders that God cares for us and will meet all our needs. That promise pervades scripture. God knows what we need and will provide it:

> If God so clothes the grass of the field, which grows today and is thrown into the oven tomorrow, will he not much more provide for you, O you of little faith? So do not worry and say, "What are we to eat?" or "What are we to drink?" or "What are we to wear?" All these things the pagans seek. Your heavenly Father knows that you need them all. But seek first the kingdom [of God] and his righteousness, and all these things will be given you besides. (Mt 6:30–33)

We simply need to ask and to receive with gratitude.

The attitude of gratitude that underlies stewardship can help with decluttering as well. On shopping outings when I'm being more spiritually aware, I'll stop to think, "I have so much. Do I need this too?" On less spiritually aware days, I just whip out the credit card. When we receive everything as gift, it is easier to share those gifts with those in need: "Without cost you have received; without cost you are to give" (Mt 10:8). Gratitude opens the heart, and an open heart leads to open hands. Open hands free us to let go of our excess and to reach out to our brothers and sisters. We can pass on our unused or underused possessions to those whose need is greater. Stewardship—the right relationship to things—liberates us from being possessed by our possessions.

The Perfect Moment

Sometimes, I'm shopping for something I need and I stumble across an amazing deal—a deal so good that I just can't pass it by. So I don't. Maybe it was a beautiful sweater or a fancy candle in my favorite scent or molded chocolates or a perfectly marbled steak. It's special, so I decide to save it for a special occasion. While I wait for that perfect moment, the purchase sits in the freezer or the cabinet or the closet or, just possibly, on the pile in the corner. I didn't pick these examples by accident. They are all things I've recently purchased that I didn't need or that I haven't used. All too often, by the time the perfect moment arrives, the steak is freezer-burned, the chocolates are stale, the candle is melted, and the sweater no longer fits. If you've never donated an article of clothing that still has the tag on it, you are a better person than I. Clutter has robbed me of the pleasure of my purchase and has wasted precious resources. That great deal doesn't look so good now; does it?

Once again, our faith teaches us how to proceed. The Greek used in scripture has two words for time: *chronos* and *kairos*. Chronos—the root of our word *chronological*—refers to the minutes, hours, and days by which we measure our lives. But Jesus often uses the word *kairos*. Kairos means the opportune moment—that perfect moment for which we save special things. Kairos is a prophetic reminder to capture and treasure each moment, living life abundantly rather than single-mindedly seeking abundance (cf. Jn 10:10). Jesus proclaimed that the opportune moment has arrived (cf. Mk 1:15). Living in the opportune moment doesn't mean that we don't save or make an effort to use our nicest things to mark special occasions. It doesn't mean that we live utterly heedless of the future. It means that we use things for their intended purposes and that we use them with joy—making every day holy. So I light the candles when I come home from work to mark the transition between work and leisure. I grill the steak on an ordinary Sunday evening, just so I can share a special meal with someone I love. Living in kairos means seeking to experience God's hand in each moment—a new way to measure our days.

My Journey

I own an antique bedroom suite. It belonged to my grand-parents originally, and four other people in my family owned it before me. (My family is big on hand-me-downs. As I look around my house, I realize that I'm the original owner of less than a third of my furniture.) One of the pieces of the suite is a large dresser with three drawers and a mirror. Unfortunately, over the years, I'd tossed so much stuff on the dresser top that I could barely see the mirror. Taking anything off the dresser threatened an ava-lanche. The top drawer had become the repository for so much junk that I didn't even remember what was in it, and finding anything was just impossible.

I finally set aside a few weeknights to get to the bot-tom of things—literally. As I took things off the dresser top and out of the drawer, I sorted them into containers on the bed so that I would know what I had. Everything went into one of the marked containers, assigned to its proper place in the house (why was there a spoon on my dresser?), or into the trash (AOL disks, anyone?). The fact that I filled more than three packing boxes can give you an idea of how much stuff was on that dresser.

Once things were sorted, I could start deciding what to keep and what should go to a new owner. Some things were easy. Apparently, I'd been tossing coins into various containers on the dresser for years. I was able to gather them into a huge jar as savings. I put all of the unexpired gift cards into a single place where I would remember to use them.

The first box held a random assortment of objects—from cords for unknown electronics to drapery hooks. Most of that could be donated or discarded.

The two biggest boxes were filled with beauty prod-ucts and jewelry. Sorting the jewelry was like Christmas!

I found dozens of pieces that I had forgotten I owned. I took the time I needed to match earrings with their mates and to put the pieces away in the now-empty top drawer. Most of my jewelry comes from one of two places: either I bought it while I was traveling or I inherited it from a family member. As I sorted the necklaces, I remembered buying one of them from an HIV-positive woman in Kenya, chatting with her as she fastened it around my neck. A pair of glass earrings reminded me of the man who sold them to me in a little shop not far from the Vatican. A beautiful pin belonged to my grandmother, and my dearest friend wore it at her wedding as her "something borrowed." So many memories in such small items! Now they rest in a place worthy of the memories they hold. As a bonus, since my jewelry is neatly organized and easily accessible, it's easier for me to put it on when I get dressed. If I discover that I'm not using some pieces, I can donate them.

Dealing with the beauty products was a bit easier. I found a ton of small bottles of toiletries, collected from hotels as I've traveled or purchased to meet security standards when I've flown with only a carry-on. Anything unopened was donated to a homeless shelter; shelters are always looking for toiletries that they can give to their clients. The partially used bottles went into the bathroom, sorted by product type. Instead of buying new shampoo, conditioner, shower gel, toothpaste, and lotion, I used up all of these partial bottles, one after another. In less than a year, I managed to cut the clutter by more than half. (And I saved money by avoiding new purchases.) The most depressing part of the process was looking at all of the expensive cosmetics I'd accumulated. I had used them once or twice and then forgotten I had them. Since partially used cosmetics can't be donated and they expire quickly, most of them ended up in the trash. What a waste! What a humbling experience! How much good could I have done with that money? What was I thinking when I made those purchases?

Seeing everything stacked in cartons forced me to face some of my challenges and admit my flaws:

- I buy things on impulse but never use most of them.
- Sometimes I buy things because I feel pressured to buy or embarrassed if I don't.
- I don't store things in easily accessible places, making it harder to use the items I have.
- Because I often can't find things, I duplicate purchases. I'm one person; I don't need four bottles of shampoo!

Once the dresser was clear, I could decide what I wanted to return to the dresser top. Instead of my dresser being a dumping ground for anything in my hand when I entered the bedroom, the top now holds practical things, such as my brushes and hair ties. I can use the remaining space to display a few small items that hold special memories of people I love and places I've been: framed photographs of my mom and dad when they were young, a carved wooden bowl purchased in Africa, a handmade leather jewelry box bought in Florence, and a small crystal swan given to me by my dearest friend.

Signposts for Your Journey

No matter how formidable the task of decluttering seems, it will never be finished until you begin. If you're anything like me, even small steps forward can create the momentum you need to make real progress. Here are some first steps that have helped me as I've begun my decluttering journey:

1. **Stop buying.** I can't emphasize this enough! The most important starting point is to stop making things worse. As much as possible, avoid bringing anything

into the house that isn't absolutely necessary. I've developed the habit of always shopping with a list and of questioning every purchase that I want to make. I don't go shopping for entertainment or just to see what's in the store. I don't look at catalogs or ads unless I'm researching a specific purchase. Instead of buying books, I put them on hold at my local public library. Until I get my current possessions under control, I don't want to add to them. As a side benefit, this practice forces me to make more productive use of the things I already own. I'm using up food in the pantry and freezer and beauty products I forgot I owned. I'm reading books that I bought years ago and never read. When I've read them, unless they become favorites, they can go into the donation bag. I'm digging clothes out of the back of my closet and from the bottom of drawers. If I don't want to wear it, that makes it easy to give away. But if I like it and I haven't worn it in years, it feels new! I can use the money I save to add to my savings or to reward myself with something that won't cause clutter, such as theater tickets.

2. **Clean something, anything.** Making some progress, no matter how small, can get you on the right path. Pick something obvious—something you pass every day that annoys you. The more annoying the clutter is, the better clearing it will make you feel. Maybe there's a drawer you have trouble closing or a cabinet that things fall out of. For me, it was the top of my dresser. Now, every morning as I get ready for work, I am reminded that progress is possible. And that reminder encourages me to pick something else to tidy—maybe the table where I put my mail or the medicine cabinet in the bathroom or the linen closet.

3. **Finish the tasks you begin.** For one month, make a point to finish every task you start. Take the trash and recycling outside. Fold the laundry and put it away. Empty the dishwasher. File the paid bills. Put the clean clothes on hangers. Getting into the habit of completing tasks will keep the unfinished tasks from adding to the clutter. After all, when the sink is already full of dishes, what's a few more? And even clean and folded laundry adds to the clutter when it's sitting on the couch. Finishing each task will also provide satisfaction. Getting rid of all my clutter is going to take months, not days. I'll see progress, but I won't be finished. But being able to look at something and say, "Well, that's done!" will help keep me going.

4. **Avoid using boxes to store the things you are organizing.** This tip may sound counterintuitive. After all, doesn't storing things in nice containers make the house look tidier? Well, yes, it does. Neatly stacked boxes look much better than random papers strewn across the dining room table. The problem is that those boxes are all too likely to become permanent homes for your clutter instead of temporary way stations. You can use containers to hold stuff as you sort it, but give yourself no more than a week to empty the box. Once things are in a box, it's way too easy to forget about them and to lose all incentive to sort everything in the box and put it where it actually belongs. And because you don't know what's in each box, finding something you need means that you have to search through multiple boxes. (I'm way too likely to get frustrated and just buy another of whatever I'm trying to find! I have boxes of recipes I've been meaning to sort, not to mention all the random stuff

I've hidden in pretty containers before guests arrived.) It's so much faster to sort things and put them where they belong while you still know what's in each box.

Thoughts for the Journey

- What possessions hold special memories for me? Is there a way to honor the memory without the possession?
- What items, if any, am I saving for a perfect moment? What would that moment be?

Try This

This week, focus on gratitude. Two or three times a day, before you make use of an ordinary possession (say, your toothbrush or a food processor or a book), take a moment to think about what this possession brings you (good health, tasty food, entertainment, or knowledge). Thank God for his loving care. At the end of the week, reflect on any changes in the way that you relate to the things you own.

3.

Clutter and Sin

I have to admit it; sometimes I feel like I'm trying to empty the ocean with a teaspoon. No matter how much I try, it seems as though my cleaning is never finished. I start decluttering the first room in my house, and by the time I finish the last room, the room I started with is cluttered again. I'm beginning to think that it's impossible for my whole house to be tidy at the same time. Even while I'm spending my precious free time cleaning one room, I'm adding more clutter to another room. Sometimes, I just shake my head and repeat St. Paul's words to the Romans: "For I do not do the good I want, but I do the evil I do not want" (Rom 7:19). Why can't I make progress? What keeps me from accomplishing the things I want to achieve?

God's Path
The Wages of Sin

Put simply, sin describes the bad things we do and the good things we don't do—in theological terms, sins of commission and sins of omission—"what I have done and what I have failed to do." The clutter I see (and trip over) in my house is a constant reminder of the sin in my life.

Let me be perfectly clear: I'm not saying that having a cluttered house is a sin. Though accumulating clutter is not sinful in and of itself, it can point to areas of sin in our lives. It is a symptom of a larger disease, but treating the symptom will help only for a while. The real cure comes when we address the underlying cause or causes. Those underlying causes are the sins that we struggle to remove from our lives. So what might those sins be? Let me give you some examples from my own life.

It's hard to ignore the effects of envy. Envy means we want what other people have. Today's highly connected society seems designed to arouse envy in our hearts. Two hundred years ago, I would have known the people in my town. Maybe I'd have had a few books or read a local newspaper that told me how other people lived. My ability to compare my life to the lives of others would have been limited. But today, media and advertising overwhelm me with images of how others live. All too often, these images promote an idealized standard, designed to make me dissatisfied with my life so that I'll buy whatever they are selling to make life "better." They tell me that if I only acquire some specific item—new clothes, a new electronic gadget, a new car—my life will be happier and more fulfilled. Of course, those promises are false. I'll be the same person, just with more stuff.

My personal downfall comes from watching Christmas movies. You know, the ones the television networks seem to start showing the week before Halloween. My problem isn't the movies themselves. The theme of those movies is always admirable: things don't make us happy—caring for the less fortunate and spending time with the people we love is the true source of long-lasting joy. No, my problem is the commercials. They all depict the perfect holiday gatherings—spacious homes with beautiful furniture and elaborate decorations, sumptuous meals served on sparkling china to elegantly dressed guests. My first reaction is "I WANT!" (Okay, sometimes I've yelled that at the screen. It scares my dog.) The envy aroused by these images makes my small house with no formal dining room, space for only a tabletop tree, and no outdoor decorations seem shabby and inadequate. That could explain why I have decorations and serving ware that I never use—purchased to support a life I wish I had. Envy, in the flesh. Envy in the attic and the cabinets.

Greed and gluttony are envy's first cousins. Greed and gluttony live by a simple motto: if one is good, more is better. Greed is why I use my precious resources to acquire more and more, even when I don't need it. Gluttony is why I eat that third slice of pizza, even when I stopped being hungry after two slices. Acquiring more, having more, makes me feel more secure, more important, more valuable. But greed and gluttony are funny things. The more I get (or eat), the less pleasure I get out of each thing. Psychology has a fancy term for that effect—hedonistic adaptation—but greed and gluttony are easier to pronounce! When I quietly eat my way through the leftover Halloween candy, that last fun-size bar is nowhere near as satisfying as the first. Yet I keep eating, trying and failing to find the same level of pleasure. On the other hand, if I save favorite foods for an occasional treat, I enjoy them more. St. John Chrysostom described it like this:

> While rich, you will never cease thirsting, and pining with the lust of more; but being freed from your possessions, you will be able also to stay this disease. Do not then encompass yourself with more, lest you follow after things unattainable, and be incurable, and be more miserable than all. (*Homilies on the Gospel of St. Matthew*, Homily 63, no. 3)

Retail establishments understand the tendency to greed and gluttony. That's the marketing theory behind most of the sales I see. Buy-one-get-one offers generally don't save me money. They entice me to buy more than I need, thinking that I'm getting a better deal. All that "more" has to go somewhere. In my case at least, it ends up in the kitchen cabinets or the closet or the attic. (Okay, the pizza actually ends up on my hips, but that's a different book!)

Greed and gluttony can also shield me from having to make a choice. It's tough to decide between the blue sweater and the red one, so I buy both. I go to the store to get a book to read on vacation, and I come home with three. It doesn't matter whether I buy them at full retail price or at a used book store. The issue is overindulgence, and clutter is the result.

Every time I start to declutter, I'm ashamed to see how much virtually unused stuff finds its way into the donate pile. In almost every case, the things I end up discarding were things acquired without much thought, just because I wanted more or couldn't choose or because there was a deal. This explains why I've been using the same five-pound bag of chocolate chips for years. It was a deal.

While greed and gluttony lead me to acquire more, sloth is a major reason that clutter builds up in my house. I mean, it's not like I don't know how to declutter. Hello! I'm writing a book about it. But the bridge between knowing and doing is washed out by sloth—and not the cute kind that live in a sanctuary in Costa Rica. (I have a problem with watching online videos.) Sloth is a type of laziness, motivated in my case by lack of energy, time, and interest. Like you, I'm a busy person. I travel a good bit and my job takes a lot of my energy. When I get home from work, sometimes it's all I can do to walk the dog, make dinner, call my mom, shower, and get to bed. On a good day, I finish the newspaper and pay the bills. But it's all too easy to leave the dinner dishes in the sink, my work clothes on the bedroom chair, and the rest of the mail on the table. And that's where things stay—often for days. And the bigger the stacks get, the longer it takes to clear them, so the less likely I am to do it. Sometimes, I have to run out of cereal bowls before I wash the dishes. When I do get around to doing some basic tidying, I only do it halfway. You know what I mean. I do the laundry, but I don't fold it or put it away. It just sits there in crumpled heaps, taunting me. I pay the bills, but I don't file the receipts, so the stacks of paper just keep growing. (I have my suspicions that they breed.)

If I can't keep up with the regular housework, it's even less likely that I'm going to set aside the time for a major decluttering project. Weekday evenings just don't allow enough time to make much headway, and I save my weekends for errands. If the weather is nice, I like to be outside as much as possible. The last thing I want to do on a gorgeous Saturday is to sit in my bedroom sorting shoes. It's just so much easier to tell myself that I'll get around to it someday. That's the sloth talking. If I'm honest, there's time. I'd just rather spend it watching videos of baby sloths.

There's one more sinful cause behind my clutter. It's the toughest to talk about because it cuts too close. I accumulate stuff because I'm afraid. I'm afraid that I won't have something when I need it. I'm afraid that I will run out. I'm afraid that I will look bad or disappoint people. I'm afraid that I will make the wrong choice. I'm afraid that I'll miss an opportunity. I'm afraid that I will fail. So much of my identity is tied up with being successful and self-sufficient. The things I acquire are building blocks in the fort that protects that image of myself. Having extras makes me feel safe.

At the heart of my fear is a lack of trust in the Providence of God. *Providence* is a word we don't use very often anymore. "Divine Providence" is just a fancy way of saying that God provides. God knows what we need and will provide for us. It may not be in the way we expect, but God provides in accordance with his plan. Now, God's plan may not be my plan. God's plan may not lead to worldly success. It may require me to do without some things I desire. God's plan might require me to graciously accept the help offered by others. But God will never abandon me, even when I forget he's there. Following God's plan will lead me to live with him forever. No worldly goods—no matter how many I acquire and store—can do that.

The Separation of Sin

Sometimes, I think I use the possessions that clutter my house as a barrier—a grown-up version of a blanket fort, keeping God and others out. The *Catechism of the Catholic Church* defines sin as "failure in genuine love for God and neighbor caused by a perverse attachment to certain goods" (CCC, 1849). Sin damages all of our relationships. When I don't rely on the Providence of God, when I start to believe that I'm all I need, it's easy to see how that attitude might affect my relationship with God rather negatively.

The more independent I need to feel, the less often I wi. turn to God in need and gratitude. I begin to forget that God is the source of all the good things in my life. I can even start to think that I don't need God. Of course, I'm wrong.

I can also use my possessions to create distance between me and other people. I buy extras of everything so I don't need to ask others for help. Our culture places a very high value on being independent, on not needing others' help. I didn't realize how odd that was until I participated in a mission trip to Kenya. One day, we visited a school and home for street children in one of the slums of Nairobi. I got to spend time with two wonderful girls, Gladys and Florence. We spent a few minutes in small talk. They told me their favorite subjects in school. I showed then pictures of my dog. They asked me how many members of my family live with me. With great pride, I told them that I have my own house and live on my own. After all, isn't that the American dream—a home of your own? But I was stunned by their reaction. They pitied me! These young girls, whose worldly possessions fit in a footlocker, pitied me because I had no one to share my life! Having a surplus of possessions might let me believe I don't need other people, but, of course, I am wrong.

Confession and Conversion

If sin is one of the reasons that we acquire clutter, it stands to reason that the spiritual practices that address sin will help us root these causes out of our lives. Now, these practices won't clean out our closets or empty the storage sheds, but they can help us break the cycle of acquiring more stuff and feeding the clutter monster. More important, these practices will bring us closer to God and help us live the call to holiness. As Pope Francis has reminded us, the very name of God is mercy. God is always extending his love and forgiveness to us; we just need to accept it.

Fully accepting God's merciful love requires conversion. The *Catechism of the Catholic Church* says that:

> Interior repentance is a radical reorientation of our whole life, a return, a conversion to God with all our heart, an end of sin, a turning away from evil, with repugnance toward the evil actions we have committed. At the same time it entails the desire and resolution to change one's life, with hope in God's mercy and trust in the help of his grace. (CCC, 1431)

Conversion is more than just a change of attitude; it requires making a change in the way we live. As persons of faith, we must strive each day to turn away from sin and to turn toward God. God will provide the grace to keep us on that path.

The Sacrament of Penance is a celebration of God's abundant mercy, yet it's a sadly underused sacrament. Receiving this sacrament includes an examination of conscience to identify our sins, confession of those sins to a priest, an expression of sorrow for those sins, accepting a penance, and absolution. Like decluttering, Penance requires that we face our failures and bad habits and that we recommit to doing better in the future. Penance helps us to achieve this goal through the help of God's grace. I sometimes wonder if I avoid Penance for the same reason that I avoid decluttering: I don't like to admit my own failures and weaknesses, and I don't want to face the hard work I need to do in order to change.

Fortunately, there are things we can do every day to help make ourselves more open to receiving God's mercy. One of the practices that I have found most helpful is the Examen. Traditionally, you do the Examen at night before going to sleep, but you can do it whenever works for you. (I tend to do it as I walk my dog. I get time for quiet reflection, and the dog gets a longer walk. We're both happy.) The practice is simple. You think through your day, looking for the moments when you felt God's presence and love and honestly assessing your own actions, considering when you responded to others with loving kindness and when you did not live the way you know you should. You conclude your reflection with a prayer of thanksgiving for God's presence, sorrow for your failures, and a commitment to try harder tomorrow. The Examen gets much of its power from the fact that, once it becomes a daily habit, it teaches you to be more attentive throughout your day. You become more aware of God's presence and begin to seek out opportunities to be kinder and more loving. It changes your focus.

Similar attentiveness can help to address some of the sins that underlie the accumulation of things that become clutter. Being attentive to how you respond to other people will naturally carry over to attentiveness to your purchases and to the ways you choose to spend your time. That attentiveness makes it easier for you to say no to acquiring more or to say yes to overcoming sloth to do the things you need to do to keep clutter at bay.

Another traditional concept that can help is to avoid near occasions of sin. Most broadly, this means staying away from people, places, and other triggers that lead you to sinful behavior. For example, a person with an addiction to pornography might install a computer filter that blocks access to problematic sites. Or a person who has a problem with anger might develop a habit of stepping away from situations when he or she feels tempers rising. The goal is to make it easier to do what is good and harder to do what is wrong.

We can take the same approach in dealing with habits that let clutter accumulate and that keep us from dealing with it. For example, I take a list whenever I shop. While I may not be perfect in keeping to the list, I'm more likely to avoid buying things I don't need. I use lists even when I'm shopping for things like Christmas gifts. When I find myself being overly tempted by the advertisements I see, I start recording shows so that I can fast forward through the commercials or I take a break from reading certain magazines. Since I know sloth is a problem for me, I can focus on completing every task I start. I can make an effort to schedule basic tasks and actually put larger tasks on my calendar, just like any other commitment.

Although I know the things I should be doing, I find that I need constant reminders to keep me on the right path. Wisely, the Church sets aside days and seasons for us to give special attention to our need for confession and conversion. The season of Lent is an extended period of time that encourages us to pare away distractions and focus on our relationship with God. I've always thought that it's especially helpful that Lent occurs exactly when I've started forgetting my New Year's resolutions and continues through spring-cleaning time!

Lent isn't a spiritually tinged self-help program. It's about renewing my baptismal commitment to become the holy person God calls me to be. But if sin underlies some of the behaviors I find problematic, God's grace supporting my conversion can help me to avoid these sins and replace them with healthy, holy habits. (We'll talk more about how the traditional Lenten practices of prayer, fasting, and almsgiving can help with decluttering in the next chapter.)

While I try to use every Lent to develop good habits, I need more regular reminders of my need to recognize sin and change my life. I can fall into a lot of bad habits between April of one year and February of the next! That's where Friday comes in. Traditionally, the Church has called people to some form of penance each Friday as a remembrance of Jesus' Death on the Cross—a death that breaks the hold of sin and lets us live in the freedom of God's children. Until the 1960s, that penance took the form of abstaining from meat. Though Catholics are no longer required to avoid meat on Fridays, we are still called to embrace some penance to help us master our tendency to sin and to incline our hearts to receive God's mercy. Some penances that might be especially meaningful include fasting from any shopping on Fridays (even online!) or giving up television, media, and other entertainment so that the time can be spent in prayer, family activities, volunteering, and/or accomplishing important tasks. The penance we need depends on the sins we are trying to master—and that may change over time. Just as all sin is personal, the penance to address it will be personal as well.

My Journey

The clothes trigger my decluttering. I'm tired of struggling to make room to put away the clean laundry. I hate it that I can't find my favorite dress because it's lost in the crush in my closet. I'm annoyed enough that I overcome my sloth and decide to deal with the excess.

As a first step, I take everything out of the drawers—even if that means I just dump things onto the (clean) floor or onto the bed. Everything has to come out. Once everything is out, I sort the clothes by type (T-shirts, sweaters, shorts, skirts, etc.). This step is a mixture of shame and discovery. I am ashamed that I have so much but thrilled when I discover clothes I didn't even remember that I'd bought. It's like getting a new wardrobe for free!

Then I start to wonder: With all of these clothes, why do I wear the same fifteen outfits to work? Sorting everything by type lets me get a sense of how much I will need to give away. I know how much storage space I have, so I can divide it between the types of clothing. Do I need sweaters more than shorts? Jackets more than slacks? Once that's decided, if I have twice as many clothes as will fit in the space available, I need to give away half of what I currently own. It's good to have a target in mind before I start.

Once I finish sorting, the hard work begins. I have to look at each piece of clothing to make sure it's in good condition and try it on to make sure it still fits. I have a habit of holding on to clothes long after I should have let them go. I just hate throwing clothes away, but stained and irreparably torn clothes just can't take up my limited storage space. Now, I'm not saying that I should throw something away because it's missing a button or has a small tear on a seam. But keeping those clothes means I have to take the time to repair it myself or pay a seamstress to repair it for me. If I'm not willing to do either of those things, do I really want to keep the item?

Trying on clothes has to be my least favorite part of decluttering my wardrobe. There's nothing more depressing than realizing that a favorite item of clothing doesn't fit anymore. Like many women, my weight has varied a lot over the years and I have clothing appropriate to all of those weights. At this moment, I have clothes in five different sizes in my closet. But getting rid of the sizes that don't fit today is always a risk. A few years ago, I decided to lose weight and gave away a lot of my larger clothes as my weight came down. But then, in the year of my father's death, I regained the weight. The new, smaller clothes I bought no longer fit, and I didn't have the larger clothes. It was so depressing to have to buy new, larger clothes.

Because I know that my weight is likely to vary, I had to develop a few rules of thumb about what I can keep:

- If it hasn't fit in the last five years, it can't stay.
- I can't keep anything that's too small today unless I'm actively doing something to be able to fit into it again. (I have a favorite pair of jeans that I use to gauge my weight. If they don't fit, I'm too heavy. If they fit, I'm doing okay. If they need a belt, I'm at goal.)
- Anything that doesn't fit now has to be stored outside my bedroom (usually in storage boxes in the attic). Keeping several different wardrobes in my room means I can't see and use the clothes that actually fit today.
- I don't give away any larger clothes until I've maintained a weight loss for at least a year.

Once I'm left with the clothes that fit, I still have to decide what to keep. I always struggle with why I don't wear certain clothes. Is it because I don't really like them or because my closet is so crowded that I forget I own them? In the latter case, thinning the closet can make it easier to make good use of everything I own. I also have to be practical about how many clothes I really need. I'm a runner. Every race I run, I get a T-shirt. Even with regular runs, I just don't need *that* many. I have to pare back the quantity at least once a year. Now, I don't even take the T-shirt for a race unless there's something special about it or I have to replace some stained shirts. If those criteria don't get the piles down to a manageable level, the final question is always, "Do I feel good when I wear this?" If the answer is no, into the donation bag it goes.

The last difficult batch of clothes to sort is the special event clothes. I have some winter clothes that I only use when I'm going to be in the snow for a while. That doesn't happen very often where I live, but I don't want to have to buy new winter clothes when it does. Similarly, I don't go to a lot of fancy events, so I don't wear my fancier dresses very often. In these cases, I keep only items I've worn in the last few years, and I store them apart from my everyday clothes.

Signposts for Your Journey

Once you've decided to declutter, it's important to get started quickly, before the momentum fades. Here are some steps to help you get started:

- Set aside a few large blocks of time to declutter a specific room or area. You can do a smaller decluttering project in a short period of time each day, but a major decluttering effort will make a big mess, at least in the short term. You may find it hard to cook dinner with your pots and pans in the middle of the kitchen floor.
- Start by taking everything out of the drawers, closets, and cabinets in the designated space. Once everything is out in the open, sort things by type (books, jewelry, shoes, etc.). It can be overwhelming to see exactly how much there is! Seeing a stack of sweaters taller than you are can help to strengthen your commitment to cut back on what you own.
- Go through each pile, dividing it into "keep," "give away," or "trash." As a general rule, you should keep only those things for which you have sufficient storage space. That means no more buying clothes that won't fit in your closet. "Trash" is anything broken, in poor condition, or hopelessly outdated (8-track tape players?). The "give away" pile will be the most diverse. That pile might include things you want to donate to charity, give to a friend or family member, send to a

consignment store, or sell online. The key to that pile is that those objects leave your house for good.

- It will probably be necessary to go through the "keep" pile more than once, winnowing the pile a little more each time until you reduce it to the desired level. A second or third pass can make it easier to decide which things you really value and which things you are keeping out of habit.

- If you aren't sure whether something belongs on the "keep" or "give away" pile, put it on a timer. If you haven't read the book, worn the shirt, or used the utensil within a specified time (say, three months), it finds a new home somewhere else. If you don't use something after three months of really trying, do you really need it?

- Once you've winnowed the pile down to what you want to keep, put things away neatly. Storing too many things in the space available makes it far more difficult to use what you have. If you have to take everything out of the drawer to get to a sweater, you're less likely to wear it. If you can see what you have, you can make the best use of what you already own instead of feeling pressured to buy more. If the things you want to keep don't fit in the space available, go through the pile one more time.

- Make sure you know where everything is stored. Make a chart if necessary. If you're like me, you often have duplicates because you forgot where you stored what you have. Assigned storage spaces solve that problem.

- Things should be easily accessible and stored where you use them. Keeping small appliances in the basement and bath salts in the hall closet makes it far less likely that you will use them. If the ice cream maker is close at hand, you're far more likely to whip up a quick batch of rocky road for a summer dessert. Unused items—even if they are in like-new shape—are clutter.

Thoughts for the Journey

- What are some of the sinful behaviors that might underlie my accumulation of clutter?
- What near occasions of sin do I need to avoid so that I can deal with my clutter?
- What forms of penance can help me learn to master my sin with God's help?

Try This

This week, focus on how the media and ads affect the way you feel about your possessions. First, consider the ways that the television shows you watch and the magazines you read might make you feel as though the things you have are inferior. Notice how sale ads trigger the urge to make a purchase immediately. Then try a media fast for one day, using the time to look at the objects you already own with new eyes.

4.

Clutter and Repentance

It's a combination of procrastination and magical thinking. I delay doing the things I need to do to get my life in order—until the New Year, until Lent starts, until I finish this project. Once the calendar turns to the selected date, I somehow convince myself that everything that has stood in the way of developing a less cluttered, balanced, more spiritual life will vanish and I'll wake up on the appointed day with the focus, commitment, and energy I need to make the changes I desire.

Of course, it rarely works out that way. I oversleep on New Year's morning and wake up to a sink full of dirty dishes from the night before. Ash Wednesday arrives and I leave for work early so I can get to Mass—but long before Holy Week, prayer is once again relegated to spare moments and I'm looking for excuses to do the things I gave up. As one project ends, another waits on deck. The selected dates come and go, but I don't make the changes

I know I need to make. I want to be a different, better person, living more simply and walking more closely with God. But how can I make the changes that last?

God's Path

No, God Isn't My Fairy Godmother

Changing my life isn't a matter of meeting an external timeline; I have to start with internal change. When I focus on the externals, at best my changes are at surface level. It's like when I try to tidy up just before company arrives. There's no time to sort things, get rid of the excess, and put everything in its proper place. So I end up shoving all the extra stuff into closets or under the bed (thank God for bed skirts!). It gets me through my company's visit, but eventually, I'll need to open the closet door and everything will come tumbling out. Nothing will have changed for the better. In fact, I may have made things worse. I won't know where to find anything, and digging through the closet will take too long. So much easier to buy another of whatever I need.

Changing for the better requires setting out on a new path. As we noted in the last chapter, in Christian understanding, this reorientation to a new path—to God's path—is called conversion. Each follower of Christ is called to conversion. But, like decluttering, conversion is not a one-time thing. It's an ongoing process. Each day, I have to strive to conform my will to God's will for me. God's grace is always present to assist me in this endeavor. God calls me, strengthens me, and offers me all the gifts I need, but I can hide his offer in the closet along with everything else for which I struggle to find a place.

Conversion begins with repentance. I have to recognize that I need to change, that I want to change, and that I am willing to do the work needed to change. God's grace is not magic, and conversion is not some sort of enchanted transformation like the fairy godmother's visit to Cinderella. (Of course, I want my conversion to last past midnight.) Making a decision to follow Christ doesn't mean that I'll wake up tomorrow and make only good decisions. It means that I'll keep trying. Repentance helps me see that I need to change. For me, repentance is often spurred when I come face-to-face with the effects of my bad choices. I look at people I have hurt or ignored. I see the times when I have failed to love. The consequences of those failures push me to change, to become the person God wants me to be.

When it comes to clutter, my need for conversion revolves around one thing: attachment. Attachment is when I cling to my possessions instead of God, trusting them to take care of me and to provide everything I need. The goal is detachment, being able to use my possessions to make my life and the lives of others easier and happier, without allowing acquiring and maintaining those possessions to become an end in itself. But that means letting go.

So how do I take the first steps? And what does this have to do with the clutter in my house anyway?

Three Steps to a Clutter-Free Home

Okay, that heading isn't really accurate, but it got you to read this, right? By its very nature, clutter is always in the way, demanding our attention. We can't ignore it when we literally trip over it every day. At the same time, keeping ourselves busy dealing with the physical reality of clutter can distract us from the sins that underlie the accumulation. What we need is a way to detach, to clear the clutter and change the habits and attitudes that let it collect.

Fortunately, the Church's Tradition includes some penitential practices that help us to detach and support the conversion we need. The practices of fasting, prayer, and almsgiving are most closely associated with Lent, but we can observe them any time. (It's not like wearing a Christmas sweater in June. No one will point and laugh.) While we don't have to practice all three at the same time, each practice reinforces the others. An intentional, periodic observance of these three practices can help us to break our attachment to things and reset our relationship with our possessions. More important, these practices help us put God back at the center of our lives. Jesus discussed these practices during his Sermon on the Mount:

> Take care not to perform righteous deeds in order that people may see them; otherwise, you will have no recompense from your heavenly Father. When you give alms, do not blow a trumpet before you, as the hypocrites do in the synagogues and in the streets to win the praise of others. Amen, I say to you, they have received their reward. But when you give alms, do not let your left hand know what your right is doing, so that your almsgiving may be secret. And your Father who sees in secret will repay you.
>
> When you pray, do not be like the hypocrites, who love to stand and pray in the synagogues and on street corners so that others may see them. Amen, I say to you, they have received their reward. But when you pray, go to your inner room, close the door and pray to your Father in secret. And your Father who sees in secret will repay you. . . .
>
> When you fast, do not look gloomy like the hypocrites. They neglect their appearance, so that they may appear to others to be fasting. Amen, I say to you, they have received their reward. But when you fast, anoint your head and wash your face, so that you may not appear to others to be fasting, except to your Father

who is hidden. And your Father who sees what is hidden will repay you. (Mt 6:1–6, 16–18)

Fasting means doing without something for a specific
period of time. Usually, we think of fasting as abstaining
from food. On a more limited scale, it might mean giving
up a favorite food or drink (such as chocolate or alcohol)
for a period of time, such as for the forty days of Lent.
But food isn't the only object of our fast. We can fast from
habits that damage our relationships—like gossip—or that
take time away from things that matter—like web surfing
for videos.

Now, spiritual fasting isn't a dieting plan. The point of
fasting isn't to lose weight or to free up more time in your
schedule. (Even though Lent happens in the lead-up to
swimsuit season, that's not the point!) In spiritual terms,
fasting has three main purposes. First, it teaches us to discipline our wills. Fasting trains us in how to say no to
ourselves. The more we deny ourselves little pleasures,
the easier it becomes to deny the bigger selfish impulses
that keep us from living in accord with God's will.

Second, fasting brings us into solidarity with those
who must do without. I have to admit it. I live a pretty
comfortable life (hence the clutter). While I don't have
everything I want, I've never gone without anything I
need. But my experience is not the norm. For all too many
people, in every country of the world, access to sufficient
food, fresh water, clothing, and housing is uncertain and
can be swept away at any moment. While the inconve-
nience and discomfort of voluntary fasting in no way
duplicates the physical pain and emotional anxiety they
experience, it can make us more sympathetic and rouse
in us a desire to be more charitable and to take action to
improve the situations of those in dire need.

Third, and most important, doing without reestablishes God's place at the center of our lives. Our hunger for food or pleasure is a faint echo of the hunger that only God can fill—a hunger for peace, meaning, and unconditional love.

This closer relationship with God leads to the second practice: prayer. Prayer lies at the heart of our relationships with God. Prayer allows us to communicate with God. We speak to God about our wants and needs, our joys and concerns, and we listen for God's response, striving to discern his will for us so that it can guide our lives. Most times, I find that talking is much easier than listening. It's easy to tell God what I want, but it's much more difficult to hear what he wants from me. Telling God what I want is an intentional act. It lets me feel as if I'm doing something. But listening requires waiting in silence. It takes time and attention. And I may hear something that I don't want to hear. The clutter in my house can keep me from finding a calm and peaceful place to pray. The clutter in my schedule can keep me from dedicating the time needed to wait for God's word. Fasting from my favorite distractions can help me open up the quiet space I need to listen. (In chapter 5, we'll look more closely at the relationship between clutter and prayer.)

God always wants the best for us, but following his will is not necessarily easy. In fact, it's almost certainly not going to be easy. Jesus warns us that following him will be accompanied by hardships and may disrupt the course of our lives: "Whoever wishes to come after me must deny himself, take up his cross, and follow me" (Mk 8:34). Following God's will calls me to follow Christ's path of humility, service, and self-sacrifice. This sacrifice is made out of love for God and neighbor, and this sacrificial love for my neighbor underlies the third penitential practice: almsgiving.

Almsgiving is an old-fashioned word for charitable donation. It refers to giving material goods—in cash or in kind—to those who are in need. But unlike some types of donation, almsgiving is motivated by love for the neighbor and a sincere concern for those who lack the necessities of life.

Dealing with clutter can inform our almsgiving in two ways. First, it can generate donations. When I get rid of all of the extra stuff in my home, I have to find a place for these things to go. It's not that these items aren't in good condition. The clothes, for example, are well made and still have lots of wear left in them. It's just that they don't fit or I don't particularly like them anymore. The same is true of kitchen gadgets (which I'm convinced multiply in the back of my cabinets). As I pare down what I own, I can donate the things I no longer need or desire to those in greater need. My excess can make up for their lack. Second, it can create spare funds. As I focus on acquiring less so that the clutter doesn't build up again, my spending will likely decrease. I can use the money I save to be more generous to those in need and to the organizations that help them. I reorient the use of my financial resources away from the selfish fulfillment (or overfulfillment) of my own desires and toward generous almsgiving.

Keeping on the Straight and Narrow

The practices of fasting, prayer, and almsgiving can help to foster conversion, allowing us to focus on our need for God, simplify our wants, and discern God's will in our lives. Still, living that conversion day in and day out can be a challenge. So how can we face that challenge? I try to follow the old maxim: Make it easy to do the right thing and hard to do what is wrong. That way, following the path of least resistance will still direct me the right way. The Church teaches similar concepts to help us live on the new path to which conversion points us: a firm amendment of purpose and avoiding the near occasion of sin. The first is a mental commitment; the second, a change in practice.

A firm amendment of purpose means that we commit ourselves wholeheartedly to a new course. We recognize that we will struggle and may even fail, but we will keep trying, giving it our best efforts. We can bolster our purpose by creating structures that help us do the right thing. Since I'm trying to deal with clutter, I might place a recycling bin next to my entryway table so that the junk mail doesn't pile up. I can keep a kitchen inventory that I can use to build my weekly grocery list so that I don't buy more than I need. I can organize my possessions so that I can find what I have and use it. If I know what I have and can put my hands on it when the moment arises, I'm less likely to end up with a three-year supply of bath salts taking up space in my bathroom closet. (For the record, the same principle applies to other things as well, including food in my pantry and craft supplies in my storage chest.)

This firm amendment of purpose requires accountability. Sometimes, I can maintain accountability on my own, for example, keeping a record of my donations to charity. But other times, I need someone to hold me accountable to my commitment. A friend might check in to make sure I'm working through the clutter as planned or may question my desire to purchase nonessentials. The accountability might be mutual. I can make a standing date with a friend to go to church or to read and discuss spiritual books.

Avoiding the near occasion of sin means staying away from people, places, and circumstances that tempt us into the behaviors that we are trying to purge from our lives.

For example, if I am trying to quell my tendency to gossip, I might avoid spending time with people whose primary topic of conversation is other people. When it comes to dealing with clutter, I have several temptations that I need to avoid, such as paging through catalogs or going shopping for entertainment, just to pass time. These behaviors make it more likely that I will end up buying things I don't need. Since I know what things I tend to buy and never use, I can take extra care to avoid stores that sell those things. I've even delegated friends to hold me accountable, steering me past jewelry displays and cosmetic counters. Similarly, if I go to a store without a list, I know that I'm coming home with things I don't need. When I have a list, if something isn't on the list, I have to walk around the store for at least five or ten minutes before buying it. Amazingly, even so short a time helps me to avoid nonessential purchases. Still, I've learned that I just can't go window-shopping. That casual act just makes me want to acquire more, using up my resources and adding to my clutter. These small denials can keep me away from the bigger pitfalls that might keep me from following the path to which God calls me—a path of generosity, love, and self-giving, following the example of Jesus.

In the end, Christianity is about encountering Jesus Christ and entering into a relationship with him and his Body, the Church. That encounter, and the resulting relationship, must change the way we live in the world as we strive to conform our lives more closely to Christ's life.

Like all conversions, we have to start with baby steps. We have to learn to tell ourselves no, to avoid making purchases, and to be happy with the things we already own. These initial steps can be simple, but that does not limit their effectiveness. During Lent, as part of my fasting, I try to avoid making any nonessential purchases. The money

I save by these small denials allows me to be more generous to those in need. The key to this strategy is defining "essential" in as limited a way as possible. Breakfast cereal and toothpaste are essential; my favorite author's newest novel is not. It also helps to devote more of my time to planning my days. This planning allows me to make better use of my time as I prioritize each day's activities. It also helps me make better use of the things I have. Planning my work wardrobe in advance lets me make better use of the clothes, shoes, jewelry, and other accessories I already own. I can also vary attire enough so that I don't get bored with what I own, driving my need to buy new things. Trying to be more intentional about all of my purchases helps me to remember that the items I own don't bring me joy.

My Journey

Once I finished the clothes, I had to face my mountains of paper and my overflowing bookshelves. Thank God for snow days, when I could spread everything out on my living room floor! Some of the papers were easily managed. Once again, I started by sorting: all the electric bills together, the receipts for each credit card in its own pile, etc. Then I organized each pile by date. I got rid of any receipt or report that was duplicated. For standard bills, I discarded everything over five years old. I did keep warranties (only for appliances I still own!), tax documentation, receipts documenting home improvements, and records I might need to prove the cost basis of some investment accounts. There was something very freeing about shredding the bank statements from the account I had in college! (I've been out of college for decades. The bank doesn't even exist anymore.) At the beginning of each year,

I can just pull a year's worth of receipts from the back of each folder and make room for the new year's records.

Personal papers are harder. I don't feel particularly sentimental about my phone bill (except remembering how inexpensive it used to be!), but that's not true of letters, programs, news clippings, and the like. Once again, I had to develop some rules of thumb to guide my decluttering:

- I don't keep photos that aren't in focus or that aren't flattering to me!
- The photos I do keep have to be labeled.
- I don't keep any cards that don't include a written note.
- I do keep handwritten letters, sorted by sender and stored in a banker's box.
- I do keep programs from live theater shows. If I have the ticket stub, I staple it to the program.
- Concert ticket stubs can stay; movie ticket stubs go.
- I keep funeral prayer cards for family members and close friends. For family members, I write the relationship on the card. It can help folks who do genealogies.
- The recipes clipped out of newspapers and magazines are sorted by food type (dessert, breakfast, vegetable, etc.). Then, I go through each one and decide how likely I am to make it. Given the number of cookbooks I own, the odds aren't good. Only the recipes I'm dying to try get saved in an accordion folder divided by type. Once I make it, if I don't love it, it's off to the recycling bin. I follow the same process with craft ideas I've cut out of magazines.

These rules usually help me reduce the paper enough to organize and store it so that I can find what I need. If I don't think I'll want or need to find a piece of paper in the future, I don't keep it!

Some keepsakes do get special treatment. I'll never *need* the letters my dad wrote to me when I was in college, but I like knowing I have them. They are memories worth keeping. So I organize them well and keep them in a place where I can look through them periodically. Strolling down memory lane is a great way to spend a lazy Sunday. And every time I go through the carton of memories, I can let a few more things go. With distance, I realize that they aren't as important as I thought they were. Sometimes, I need to be gentle with my decluttering and let time make it easier.

But then I come to the books. People who think print is dead should come to my house! I could stock a small, but eclectic, bookstore. Some of the books I have are reference books that I use for work and writing. Obviously, I have to keep those. Then, there are the personal favorites that I read at least once a year. They have to stay. I keep any book that's signed by the author. Plus, I collect old prayer books. But that still leaves hundreds of books that I must consider. And only a few are books that disappointed me so much that it's easy to say goodbye.

I love books. They were my first friends. They are still the friends I want to be with on a rainy day. Giving them away can be wrenching, like abandoning a loved one. The only thing that makes it possible for me is to be very intentional about where the books go. Some books, I've given to friends who I know will treasure them. Others, I've donated to school or church libraries. The remaining books that I need to donate go to my local library's used bookstore. Of course, that donation is a two-edged sword. All too often I take a bag of books to donate and end up buying more books!

If I'm not sure about whether it's time to let a book go, I reread it. If it still makes me happy and I find myself turning the pages eagerly, it goes back on the shelf. When I don't look forward to rereading it again, it's time to go. In the most recent declutter, I was finally able to donate three books I've had for almost ten years. I'm also trying to read the books I've bought or received as gifts that I've just never found the time to read. (There are so many good books! Thank you for reading this one!) At the beginning of each year, I place five or six of these books on a special shelf. By the end of the year, they are either read or gone—or both! Now, if I could just stop buying their replacements!

Religious books are a special challenge. I would never throw a Bible or prayer book into the trash or recycling bin. A religious book should be burned or buried. Burning books frightens me, so my options are limited. If the book is still in good condition, I will share it with someone who needs it or with a school or church library. If I can't find it a home, I keep it until I can. I've often thought that churches should collect these books and either donate them to mission churches or bury them when celebrating funerals. I know that I'd love to be buried with a few Bibles so that my earthly body would mingle with the Word of God!

Signposts for Your Journey

Getting your paper under control can jump-start your decluttering efforts. Clearing the stacks of paper off desks, counters, and tables can make a huge difference in your perception of clutter. Plus, there's something very therapeutic about feeding paper into the shredder! (Try it after a bad day at work!) One key is to limit the paper that comes into your house. Ask to be taken off mailing lists for groups you don't support, or call companies and ask them to stop sending their catalogs. If it doesn't come into your house, it will never be clutter. For things that do come into the house, keep a recycling bin near where you open the mail. Toss the junk mail you can't avoid into it immediately. It's great to keep the shredder there, too, so you can destroy anything with personal information (such as credit card applications).

There will be papers you need to keep: tax records, receipts, warranties, and the like. They require a filing system in an accessible place. If you can't find a piece of paper when you need it, why bother keeping it? You should consult a financial planner, lawyer, or tax preparer to ask how long you should keep various types of records. Other than tax returns, deeds, loan payoffs, and legal papers, very little needs to be kept more than five years. So let go of the electric bill from 1999! Make sure that you shred anything with personal information. If you have a lot of papers that need to be shredded, you will have to do it in several sessions because most home shredders overheat within ten minutes. However, some communities have low-cost or free shredding opportunities where industrial shredders can eliminate your papers in seconds and the resulting pulp is recycled!

Even if you keep your paper under control by going digital, you aren't home free. Digital systems create their own sort of clutter. Even though they aren't typically visible to people who visit your home, think about the following: your computer files, memory cards, e-mail inboxes, cloud storage, and cell phone. Because the storage is virtually unlimited, we don't feel the same pressure to declutter these. Still, at its heart, clutter isn't about the space available. Just like buying a bigger house doesn't mean that your clutter problem is resolved, just adding more cloud storage won't address your digital clutter. If you can't find the things you need when you need them, clutter is a problem.

When you are in the mood to spend some time on the computer, instead of watching videos or playing games, you can spend thirty minutes or so tackling the digital clutter:

- Delete the e-mails you no longer need, the photos that are blurred, and the apps you don't use.
- Tag photos so that you know where and when they were taken and who is in them. Organize the pictures you want to keep into clearly labeled digital albums.
- Go through the files you have stored in the cloud and on your computer, deleting those you no longer need. Rename any mystery files with titles that are easily understandable. Group related files together in clearly labeled folders.
- Review your digital subscriptions, such as e-mail advertisements and newsletters, to decide which you can cancel. I still get notices about races in Puerto Rico because I once registered for a 5K race there. Cancelling the unnecessary subscriptions will help reduce the future buildup of digital clutter.

Other things you might want to declutter include the refrigerator door and bulletin boards. I've found magnetic calendars for 2001 and take-out menus for restaurants that closed years ago! Since these tend to be relatively small areas, it's easy to take everything off and decide which things you want to repost.

Thoughts for the Journey

- What do I need to give up for a short time to help me hunger for God and feel closer to the poor?

- What things distract me from prayer and keep me from discerning God's will?
- How can I be more generous with my time, treasure, and talent? What limits my generosity?
- What places, people, or stresses encourage me to acquire more things? What changes can I make in my daily life to avoid those or to limit their influence?
- Who can help to hold me accountable to these changes?

Try This

Choose one change to implement this month. At the end of the month, check in with an accountability partner (or your journal) to gauge your progress and identify stumbling blocks.

5.

Clutter
and Prayer

Sometimes, my decluttering efforts seem positively biblical. In the beginning, there is chaos. Then we have some prophetic wailing, and crying out, "Why, O God?" and "How long, O Lord?" I beg for fire and brimstone to rain down and obliterate the clutter from the earth—or at least from my floor. After sufficient wailing, I get down to the work of separating the weeds from the wheat. The painful part begins when the time arrives to sacrifice the excess. That initial purge is followed by an extended period of building a system that will allow me to maintain the new order. Alas, this effort is plagued by many setbacks. Ultimately, I strive to arrive and live forever in the heavenly house, where there is no clutter or confusion.

If my efforts follow biblical patterns, is it such a surprise that I find the process of decluttering akin to prayer?

Of course, that means that the same obstacles that hinder my prayer life can make decluttering a challenge as well.

God's Path
Pray Through the Mess

There's no way around it, decluttering is time-consuming and repetitive. Shredding stacks of papers that contain personal information, matching the tops and bottoms of plastic containers, folding clothes—none of these tasks really requires all of my attention. But the rhythm of doing the same thing over and over frees my mind for reflection. I can recall all of the people who have asked for my prayers, commending them to God's care. I can think through my day, looking for the ways God was present. I can examine my actions, honestly assessing whether I responded positively to the opportunities to live according to God's law of love and asking forgiveness for the times I failed. Or I can just rest in the silence, sitting in God's presence and listening for his word and his will.

Decluttering done right is always difficult. While I absolutely have to get rid of clothes that no longer fit or are irreparably damaged, the books that I'll never read, and the excess papers that overflow from my files, that's not enough. That will only be a start for the decluttering that needs to be done. If I really want to reduce the clutter in my house, I have to give away some things that are still usable, maybe even some things that I still use and enjoy—the books that I might want to read again and the adorable shoes that I just don't wear that often, the kitchen utensils that I use on rare occasions. It's hard to let go of things I like. Saying no to something bad is far easier than choosing between two goods.

But if decluttering were easy, it would be less of an aid to my spiritual growth. Giving away my excess helps me to develop the detachment to which Christians are called. Jesus speaks of this detachment several times in the Gospels. During the Sermon on the Mount, he encouraged his listeners to value the lasting things of heaven over the passing things of earth:

> Do not store up for yourselves treasures on earth, where moth and decay destroy, and thieves break in and steal. But store up treasures in heaven, where neither moth nor decay destroys, nor thieves break in and steal. For where your treasure is, there also will your heart be. (Mt 6:19–21)

In other places Jesus cautioned his disciples that following him would not be an easy path. They would have to forego many physical comforts and the security they can bring: "Foxes have dens and birds of the sky have nests, but the Son of Man has nowhere to rest his head" (Lk 9:58). Complete dedication to the way of Jesus would require giving up everything. As Jesus told the rich young man who asked him how to gain eternal life, "Go, sell what you have, and give to [the] poor and you will have treasure in heaven; then come, follow me" (Mk 10:21).

This detachment from worldly goods was accompanied by a promise. Jesus assured his disciples that, while they would give up the security of their possessions, God would never abandon them. God knows our needs better than we do, and he will always provide for us. St. Thérèse of Lisieux taught a form of spirituality called "the little way." In her advice to novices, included as an appendix to her autobiography, *The Story of a Soul*, she wrote "'Remaining little' means—to recognize one's nothingness, to await everything from the Goodness of God." The sorrow and even emotional pain I feel when I let go of the possessions that clutter my house reminds me of how far I have to go in developing the detachment that discipleship requires. The sacrifice that I feel when I pass these belongings on to a new owner helps me burn through the attachment that binds me to my possessions.

Sorting possessions to decide what to give away is easiest when accompanied by prayer. Only love for God and a wholehearted willingness to rely on him can make it easy to part with the things I own. Prayer makes it easier to open my heart to the freedom that comes when I let go of things that tie me to this world instead of helping me keep my focus on God.

In the second chapter, we noted that a healthy and holy relationship with our possessions is marked by stewardship. As stewards, we receive everything we have as the gift of a loving God. Because it is a gift, we receive it with gratitude. We realize that we have not earned the good things that God has given us. In the same way, those who lack these gifts are not being punished by God. Thus, the prayer that will best accompany our efforts to deal with clutter and let go of our excess is a prayer of thanksgiving. Indeed, "thanksgiving characterizes the prayer of the Church" (CCC, 2637). As disciples, thanksgiving should be part of our daily living. And no part of our daily lives is immune from this prayer because "every event and need can become an offering of thanksgiving" (CCC, 2638).

As I sort through the piles of belongings to decide what I will keep, a prayer of thanksgiving can remind me of God's provident goodness. While I pack up the things that are easy to discard, I can give thanks that God has blessed me so that I can give generously from my excess to those in need. Prayers of petition for those who will use these objects can accompany the donation. But I find prayer most helpful when I must part with possessions that I love. Sometimes circumstances require that I let go of things in which I still find pleasure. In those painful instances, I thank God for the gift of this object and recall with gratitude the memories that the object evokes. Then, with great thanksgiving for God's love, shown in Jesus' self-sacrificial love on the Cross, I can let go of the object. It still won't be easy, but gratitude and prayerful reflection on Christ's love can open my heart and my hands.

One of These Things Is Much Like the Other

Like prayer, decluttering is often a solitary activity. (In fact, an announcement that it's time to clean the closet or the basement or the garage is virtually guaranteed to empty the house—of its occupants at least.) We may get help from a family member or friend. In some cases, we may even require the assistance of a professional. Despite the fact that we often deal with clutter alone, like prayer, decluttering always has a communal dimension. In the next chapter, we will look at the ways our clutter can have an impact on people we will never meet. Our decisions as consumers, voters, and just as inhabitants of this planet will always affect others, especially the poor. Similarly, even the most private prayers we hold in the depths of our hearts affect the whole Church. Even if we never speak them out loud, even to ourselves, they have a communal dimension. I always pray as part of the Body of Christ, joining my prayer to Jesus' eternal prayer to the Father.

Given that prayer and decluttering have so much in common, is it any wonder that many of us face the same challenges in accomplishing them? The most obvious challenge is finding time. A healthy prayer life requires that we commit to going to Mass every Sunday—even when we'd rather sleep late. More than that, we have to dedicate time for prayer every day. The key is that this time has to be part of our regular daily routine. Left to our own devices, we're all too likely to give prayer the last few minutes before we fall asleep. Or we might only pray when we're in need. That sounds a lot like how I deal with clutter. I'll tidy something for a few minutes while I'm on the phone or if I'm waiting for something, but I won't make any real effort. Or I'll postpone my decluttering plans time and again, finding any number of "urgent" things I need to accomplish instead. Then, when the need is great (the guests are coming tomorrow!), I'll declutter with great fervor and little focus. If I think that prayer and decluttering matter, why aren't they part of my daily routine? Why do I act as though they aren't worth my time?

Distraction is another challenge to both prayer and decluttering. I always start praying with the best of intentions. Maybe I even go to church to sit in the presence of the Blessed Sacrament to meditate on scripture or just listen for God. Before I know it, I'm thinking about my grocery list or a troublesome work project or what I need to tell my mom when she calls. I try to quiet my mind and focus on prayer, but my brain keeps exploring every detour it can find. I'm the only person I know who flunked a class in contemplative prayer! I just couldn't make my brain be still.

I find the same challenge in dealing with clutter. I get distracted so easily! I'll start sorting books or magazines and end up reading. Instead of shredding or filing papers, I'll start calling companies with questions about my accounts. As I declutter the closet, I'll stop to do some mending or try on outfits or plan next week's wardrobe for work. Or I'll start cleaning several different areas but never finish any of them. You know how it goes. You're cleaning the home office and you find the plate and glass you left on the desk after your snack, so you take them to the kitchen to put them in the sink. You realize that you need to do the dishes, but when you get the dish soap from the cabinet, you remember that you need to change the light bulb in the bathroom. And it goes on from there. Your desk never does get cleared. None of these distractions are bad in themselves, but they all draw us away from our goals. Both our prayer lives and our decluttering efforts need us to focus and to discipline our minds and wills to resist distractions. The *Catechism* teaches a way to do this:

> To set about hunting down distractions would be to fall into their trap, when all that is necessary is to turn back to our heart: for a distraction reveals to us what we are attached to, and this humble awareness before the Lord should awaken our preferential love for him and lead us resolutely to offer him our heart to be purified. (*CCC*, 2729)

A final similarity between prayer and decluttering stems from the fact that progress is often hard to make and even harder to see. I pray for what I need or want, but God doesn't seem to hear my prayer. I try to be a better person, but I fall into the same sinful behavior time and again. I listen for God's voice, but I'm met with silence. I suppose that I should be comforted by the fact that so many saints experienced periods (sometimes years) when they prayed without consolation, never confident that God could hear them. The word for this experience is dryness. It happens "when the heart is separated from God, with no taste for thoughts, memories, and feelings, even spiritual ones" (*CCC*, 2731). In these moments, we must cling "faithfully to Jesus in his agony and in his tomb" (*CCC*, 2731). Maybe I should consider myself fortunate to share this experience with St. Teresa of Calcutta and St. John of God. Or I can recall an answered prayer or an especially moving liturgy that seemed to speak to my soul. I can use the confidence and comfort from those moments to keep moving forward.

In the same way, sometimes it's hard to see progress with my decluttering efforts. Everything I clean just makes me aware of how much more there is to do. Sorting through clothes adds to my mending pile. Gathering photos means I need to identify them and organize them into albums. If they are older, they need to be scanned first. Moving unused suitcases from the guest room to storage just reminds me that I need to clean the attic too. It's hard to stay committed when the effort seems unending and is not rewarded. Staying the course is a challenge. It helps to look at the long term. I remember where I've come from, and I focus on where I'm going. I look back at small successes and try to build on them. In dealing with clutter, before-and-after photos of individual spaces can give me the inspiration I need to keep going. Or there might be one spot that I can keep organized, where I can always find the things that are supposed to be there. These moments can serve as refueling stations when the tank of enthusiasm runs dry.

Spiritual Hoarding

The example of clutter can also teach us about a spiritual danger. In the preface, we looked at the difference between the general malaise of clutter that many of us fight and the more serious problem of hoarding. The hallmarks of hoarding include an inability to distinguish between trash and treasure and an often-violent unwillingness to discard things, no matter how useless they may have become. Hoarding inhibits the activities of everyday life.

The spiritual life has a parallel to hoarding, though we often don't recognize it as such. Spiritual hoarding can show up in many ways. Perhaps we build our spiritual lives by adding devotions and other practices. Experiencing many types of prayer can help when our usual prayers seem dry and tedious; the variety can help us explore different parts of the Church's tradition, opening our hearts and minds to the universality of the Church. But we must be vigilant to ensure that the externals do not overwhelm our relationship with God: "In praying, do not babble like the pagans, who think that they will be heard because of their many words" (Mt 6:7). Or we can fill our time by volunteering for every church committee and ministry and attending every possible event. Certainly, parishes could not survive without their dedicated volunteers and most active parishioners. However, these activities can also hide the possibility that our relationship with God does not have any impact on our lives outside the church. It's easy to confuse the external trappings of devotion and participation with the interior conversion that must be at the center of Christian life. Jesus cautioned against this confusion when he chastised the scribes and the Pharisees:

> The scribes and the Pharisees have taken their seat on the chair of Moses. Therefore, do and observe all things whatsoever they tell you, but do not follow their example. For they preach but they do not practice. They tie up heavy burdens [hard to carry] and lay them on people's shoulders, but they will not lift a finger to move them. All their works are performed to be seen. They widen their phylacteries and lengthen their tassels. . . .
>
> Woe to you, scribes and Pharisees, you hypocrites. You pay tithes of mint and dill and cummin, and have neglected the weightier things of the law: judgment and mercy and fidelity. [But] these you should have done, without neglecting the others. Blind guides, who strain out the gnat and swallow the camel!

> Woe to you, scribes and Pharisees, you hypocrites. You cleanse the outside of cup and dish, but inside they are full of plunder and self-indulgence. Blind Pharisee, cleanse first the inside of the cup, so that the outside also may be clean.
>
> Woe to you, scribes and Pharisees, you hypocrites. You are like whitewashed tombs, which appear beautiful on the outside, but inside are full of dead men's bones and every kind of filth. Even so, on the outside you appear righteous, but inside you are filled with hypocrisy and evildoing. (Mt 23:2b–5, 23–28)

All the spiritual hoarding in the world cannot hide an unconverted heart from the God who sees all hearts.

One of the signs that spiritual hoarding might be a problem is the effect that it has on the rest of your life. If you use the externals of your spiritual devotion as a reason for not fulfilling your commitments to the people in your life, you might be a spiritual hoarder. I'm reminded of the character of Mrs. Jellyby in Charles Dickens's *Bleak House*. She was so concerned with her charitable project that she ignored the needs of those around her, even her own children. In the same way, if I am concerned about whether the purificators have enough starch to the exclusion of other serious concerns, I must reevaluate how I live my relationship with Christ and his Body.

Another sign that you might be a spiritual hoarder is the way you feel if asked to step aside from a position or ministry or to change the way that something is done. If you react with anger or depression that someone is taking away "your ministry," it's time to step back and focus on your relationship with Jesus. I've gone through periods when I needed to be involved in everything, making sure that my contributions were noticed and valued appropriately. Any suggestion that I let someone else take charge or that I step aside and let someone else have a turn felt like a threat to my identity. Like a hoarder with her treasures, I couldn't let go. Sometimes, I need to let go of even good and useful opportunities so that I can be open to even better ways to serve.

My Journey

The hardest thing for me to declutter wasn't a closet or my attic (how hard is it to throw away the boxes for appliances you no longer own?), or even my books. The hardest thing to declutter was my calendar. I don't deal well with down time. I feel that if I'm not constantly busy, I'm wasting time. Having unscheduled, unstructured time in my day is a sign that I'm not using my time well. I'm constantly afraid that I'll miss an opportunity or an experience. That means that I often take on too much. I'm running from one thing to the next, overscheduled and hectic. With all the rushing from one thing to the next, it can be difficult to truly enjoy the experiences I'm collecting. I'm just too tired and distracted. The need for constant busyness is compounded by the fact that I hate to say no to people. Maybe I'm afraid that I'll disappoint them or that they won't like me anymore. Whatever the reason, I find it very difficult to claim my own time. As I grow older and my energy naturally diminishes a bit, I'm finding it harder and harder to keep up the pace, to do all the things I want to do and all the things I should do.

Decluttering my calendar is more difficult than most other forms of decluttering because the decisions are harder. Most days, it's not that I'm choosing between good and bad. I'm not deciding "Should I go to work today, or should I stay home so that I can vandalize the neighborhood park?" I'm usually choosing between two goods: "Do I volunteer on the parish liturgy committee, or do I spend that time with my godson, teaching him his prayers and giving his mom some rest? Do I clean out that closet, or do I go for a long run?" How do I balance the work I need to do to stay employed, give back to my community, dedicate time to being a good friend, take time to pray, and still keep the house tidy and have time to sleep? The demands are infinite, but neither my time nor my energy are.

My calendar decluttering is a work in progress. I'm still overcommitted and overwhelmed by all the things I ought to be doing—not to mention the things I want to be doing. My to-do list is like some mythical beast. I cross off one thing and three more appear! But oddly, if I get to the bottom of the list with too much time left, I get nervous. Did I forget something I'm supposed to do? Am I being lazy? Am I wasting time? The only way to manage those questions is to set priorities. I have to decide which things are most important to me this day, this week, this month, and give them first call on my time. Once these priorities claim time in my schedule, I can divide the rest of my hours among the tasks that remain.

I'm trying to use some of the same methods that I used to declutter my closets and drawers to deal with my schedule. First, I'm striving to get rid of the trash that takes up too much space in my day, things such as mindless channel surfing and watching the same online video time and again. My personal nemesis is the time I waste in the morning, scrolling through my social media feeds. When I don't pick up my phone before I get out of bed, I can accomplish a myriad of tasks while I'm energetic in the morning—and thus open time for the rest of the day. I can use that newfound time to tackle the jobs that I claim are my priorities. I've started charging my phone in a place where I can hear it if it rings but where I have to get out of bed to check my feeds. That makes it easier to do the right thing.

When I declutter, I try to find things that fill multiple purposes so I can save space. I can try to do the same thing in decluttering my schedule. For example, I can volunteer for a good cause with a friend so that we can spend time together. I can plan my menus or do basic chores, like ironing, while I watch television shows I've recorded. This practice gives me two uses for the same time.

When I deal with clutter, I try to use all of the available space well. I'm trying to do the same thing with my time. While dinner is cooking, I can sort my mail, take out the trash and recycling, or clean out the fridge. While I wait for a friend to arrive to go out to a movie, instead of flipping through the television channels or surfing the web, I can pay bills or do some filing. I always carry a book or magazine so that I can read while standing in line or waiting at the doctor's office. I even pray Morning Prayer while I take the subway to work in the morning and Evening Prayer on the way home.

But these methods aren't enough on their own. Really tackling my calendar clutter requires developing new life skills. First, I'm learning to do things in small amounts rather than only tackling tasks when I can devote a lot of time to them. While I still love having large blocks of time to do things, I'm attempting to use smaller amounts of time each day to consistently chip away at bigger tasks. That helps to deal with my natural tendency toward procrastination. Second, I'm learning to find peace in saying no to requests and opportunities. A big part of that learning is humility. I have to accept that I can't do everything. I have to make choices, and every choice closes a door. Finally, I'm learning to give myself permission to relax and just be. As some friends regularly remind me, "Mary, you're a human be-ing, not a human do-ing!" Scheduling time to relax is a new endeavor for me. And like decluttering, it's a process.

Signposts for Your Journey

One of the reasons that decluttering is so difficult is that the need to declutter often coincides with emotionally difficult events. Perhaps the last child has set up her own household and now you face an empty nest. Or retirement from a life of work means downsizing to a smaller house or apartment, coupled with the loss of the part of your identity that was tied to your job. You may be moving to a new community where you will need to rebuild your professional and social circles while striving to maintain old ties. Maybe your health situation means that you need to move into a care facility, not only limiting the possessions you can keep but your independence as well. You may be a friend or family member helping in one of these situations or decluttering the home of a loved one who has died.

Helping someone declutter takes a special kind of patience. While you can help with carrying and sorting, taking out the trash and packing things to be moved or donated, the decisions about what to keep and what to discard are not yours. While you want to stay on task, it's important to leave time to listen to the stories that will arise and to honor the memories recalled by the process. Hurrying past the stories will only make the process more painful.

These difficult situations don't really change the first part of the process you use for decluttering. You still have to take everything out and sort it into "keep," "give away," and "trash." The big difference is that the amount of stuff the person you are helping can keep is far smaller. You are no longer trying to fit the possessions into the space available but into a much smaller space. Some of the decisions will be easy. If you or a loved one is moving into an assisted living or care facility, you won't need to keep kitchen utensils and the lawn mower. But you will want to keep the things needed to make a place feel like home. Then, instead of organizing what you do keep and putting it away, you must pack it for moving.

The process isn't the problem—the emotions are. Each of these situations is tied to some loss. The fact that you need to get rid of possibly cherished possessions only intensifies that feeling. Giving away your now-grown child's old ice skates may seem like a no-brainer—after all, they don't fit anyone anymore. But putting them in the donate pile means accepting that he's no longer the same little boy you drove to hockey practice every morning. Donating your work wardrobe may help a woman transitioning into the work force, but it requires exploring the parts of yourself that you have avoided in the busyness of your work life. Giving away the living room furniture because it won't fit in your new place means facing that you will never return to the home where you lived your marriage and raised your family.

Other tensions may arise as well. In all too many cases, distributing possessions can reignite family disputes. Siblings, children, and cousins can fight about who gets what and who has been favored in the distribution. Parents can be hurt when their children reject an offer to take particular possessions such as heirloom furniture, family jewelry, or special decorations. It can feel as if they are rejecting the family memories tied to those items.

There is no simple organizing technique that can make these situations easier. Loss is painful. The perfect storage system won't change that. This is when prayer can help. The psalms give us words to express our pain, fear, loneliness, and abandonment. But they also remind us that God is always with us. We can ask God to give us strength and to bring peace to our families. We can accept the inevitable, painful losses as a cross that we must bear.

Thoughts for the Journey

- What are some unexpected places that clutter develops in your life?
- What things keep you from decluttering? From prayer? How have you tried to address these?
- What do you hoard in your home? In your spiritual life?

Try This

For a specific period of time, preferably at least a month, fast from buying anything that is not consumable. That means you can buy food, go to movies, purchase services (haircuts, newspaper subscriptions, etc.), and borrow books and videos from the library, but you can't bring anything into your house that is intended to stay there. Highlight these transitions by saying a prayer of thanksgiving when you bring something into the house and a prayer when the thing is consumed or returned. At the end of the month, journal or talk with your accountability partner about the challenges you faced and what you learned.

6.

Clutter and the
Common Good

One of the things that makes dealing with clutter so difficult is that it is so personal. It's my stuff in my space. Only I can decide what's valuable and what can be discarded or given away. Often, my things are at once tied to my past, my present, and my future.

But what if clutter is bigger than that? What if it relates to the people around me? To people I don't even know? To the earth? To God? What if clutter has an impact on the network of relationships we call "the common good"?

God's Path
How Common Is the Good?

For most of us, Baptism is the moment that begins our life in the Christian community. Baptism makes us part of the Christian community by making us part of the Body of Christ. As part of this one body, we are united with all of the other members. In a very real way, we depend on them and vice versa. None of us can go it alone. We are all in this life together, and when we help one another and look out for one another, the whole body is stronger. This reality underlies our understanding of the common good.

What does the Church mean when it talks about the common good? The common good is the network of social relationships—including the government, the economy, the culture, etc.—that ought to make it possible for all members of society to fulfill their human potential. Whether or not people are baptized, concern for their well-being is part of the common good.

The common good requires three things. First, it requires respect for the dignity of human persons. This dignity comes from being made in the image and likeness of God. If anyone doesn't respect the dignity of each person or of a specific group of people, we are all diminished. Second, the common good requires that each person have access to those things needed to live in accord with that dignity. The fact that some people lack freedom or the basic necessities of life damages the common good. Finally, the common good requires peace. Obviously, if people do not feel safe—whether because of external threats or internal instability—they cannot do the things needed to fulfill their potential. (See CCC, 1905–1912.) Anything we do that impacts any one of these three things affects the common good either positively or negatively. There is no neutral activity when we operate within these cultural and social spheres of human existence.

As a members of the Body of Christ, supporting the common good is part of our mission. In his masterful encyclical on the environment, On Care for Our Common Home—Laudato si' (LS), Pope Francis teaches that conversion "entails a loving awareness that we are not disconnected from the rest of creatures, but joined in a splendid universal communion. As believers, we do not look at the world from without but from within, conscious of the bonds with which the Father has linked us to all beings" (*LS*, 220). So, as followers of Christ, we must look beyond ourselves in every decision that we make. That includes decisions about what we buy and how we deal with the clutter in our lives. Back in chapter 3, we looked at how clutter can close us off from other people. We fill our lives with stuff so that we don't have to depend on others. I can convince myself that I can take care of myself, that I am independent. The common good exposes this worldview as a lie. We are always part of the bigger picture, an interconnected world where no one is completely alone.

While I'm part of this interconnected world, I still can control only my own actions. But that doesn't give me an excuse for doing nothing or for considering only how my decisions will affect *me*. My faith calls me to broaden my worldview. Pope Francis has spoken most eloquently of the dangers present in our world, most notably exaggerated individualism. When my needs and the needs of those closest to me are the only things that matter—the only things I consider in making decisions — I betray the common good. Because I do not exist in isolation, that betrayal means that humankind suffers in some way. In *Laudato si'*, Pope Francis wrote,

> Disinterested concern for others, and the rejection of every form of self-centeredness and self-absorption, are essential if we truly wish to care for our brothers and sisters and for the natural environment. These attitudes also attune us to the moral imperative of assessing the impact of our every action and personal decision on the world around us. (*LS*, 208)

Although I strive to make decisions that align with the moral principles the Church has taught me from my youth, it's easy to forget that my actions have effects outside my small circle of family and friends. I'm just one person. How much difference can my decisions make? Certainly it's true that my personal decisions to reduce clutter or limit spending or live more simply won't reverse climate change or end the scourge of hunger. But each of us can have an impact on a smaller scale. My donations of extra furniture, bedding, and household items to a refugee resettlement agency can help newcomers create a home. The clothes I never wear can provide a working wardrobe and a confidence boost to a woman transitioning from prison to society.

Even the small changes I make support my conversion and attune me more and more to the needs of others. And this conversion is contagious. As Pope Francis stated,

> We must not think that these efforts are not going to change the world. They benefit society, often unbeknown to us, for they call forth a goodness which, albeit unseen, inevitably tends to spread. Furthermore, such actions can restore our sense of self-esteem; they can enable us to live more fully and to feel that life on earth is worthwhile. (*LS*, 212)

As Pope Francis teaches, we shouldn't discount the power of a good example. One of the great benefits of social media is the fact that it allows the easy sharing of ideas across vast spaces and through different communities. Hardly a week goes by when some act of kindness doesn't "go viral," inspiring even distant people to take similar action. While this handful of actions gets attention, countless other acts of kindness operate on a local scale only, tipping the balance toward the common good.

Stop the World; I Want to Get Off

Anyone who logs on to social media, turns on the television, or picks up a newspaper has to realize that the search for the common good doesn't seem to motivate our political and economic systems. Pope Francis has identified the cultural conditions that foster the increase in clutter and damage the common good: "Since the market tends to promote extreme consumerism in an effort to sell its products, people can easily get caught up in a whirlwind of needless buying and spending" (*LS*, 203). The world's markets are based on continued consumption. This consumption supports production and is, in turn, supported by the financial markets. The constant buying that underlies the market system clearly adds to our clutter.

Through advertising and peer pressure, we are encouraged to buy more. We continually upgrade our purchases, buying the newest, most advanced versions of various items. We are expected to grow bored with our current possessions and buy new things to renew our interest. In some cases, we have to replace possessions that are not engineered for a long life or easy repair, all the better to support the market. This desire to buy more and more ensures that our closets and cabinets remain full. But a lack of clutter doesn't necessarily mean that we're immune from this disease. Some people are serial declutterers. They purge their closets and storage areas periodically to make room for new purchases, endlessly repeating the cycle to feed their need to keep buying.

Pope Francis has called attention to this throwaway culture. In a throwaway culture, utility is the only value. Anything not immediately useful must be discarded and replaced. Viewing our possessions in this light can lead to overproduction and packed landfills. It fuels the consumption that can result in clutter. But it is even more dangerous when it extends to people. In that case, people's value does not depend on their innate dignity as a child of God but on their usefulness. A person who is no longer or not yet "a productive member of society" has no value and can be ignored or even discarded.

The Lord Hears the Cry of the Poor

The constant purchases and the accumulation that lead to clutter have numerous negative impacts on the common good. First, the need to buy more consumes the time we have available to assist those who are in need. If I add together the time I spend looking at ads, shopping online, and actually wandering through stores, not to mention the time it takes to organize and maintain all of the stuff I own, I'd probably have enough time to make a real difference. I could spend that time cleaning up trash in my community, helping out with a project in my parish, spending time with my family and friends, being still and praying, or even just resting. Second, acquiring and maintaining extra possessions requires money. That money could be shared with those who are less fortunate or used to support important projects in my parish or community.

Most important, the same economic factors that lead to clutter disproportionately affect the poor in detrimental ways. The pressure to keep prices low (to encourage more buying) and profits high forces companies to keep wages and production costs low. All too often, the workers who make the items that clutter our homes, from fast fashion to knick-knacks, and workers who staff the stores that sell these things to us receive low wages and have uncertain hours, making it difficult for them to support their families financially and emotionally. Workers in many countries are forced to accept near-slave wages, working extremely long hours while receiving few protections from workplace dangers and exploitation. Human rights agencies have filed numerous reports of workers exposed to toxic chemicals without protection or required to work in unsafe spaces and at a pace that increases the risk of a serious accident. Is my ability to buy shoes for half price worth the human cost?

My consuming more than my share means that less is available for others, especially those in greater need. Peter Maurin, who founded the Catholic Worker Movement together with Servant of God Dorothy Day, was well known for saying that the extra coat in a person's closet belonged to the poor. Peter Maurin didn't invent this saying. In fact, he was echoing a sentiment that the Church Fathers had expressed more than fifteen hundred years before. In the fourth century, a man now known as Basil the Great served as a bishop in Asia Minor. In one of his sermons that has survived, Basil spoke quite harshly to the more affluent members of his congregation. Reminding them that everything they possessed was a gift from God, he told them that the extra food, clothing, and money that they stored and protected were stolen from the poor. He did not object to people keeping the goods necessary to meet their own needs and the needs of their families. It was the excess that rightly belonged to the poor.

St. Benedict, the great founder of monasticism in the West, enshrined this principle in his famous *Rule*, which still guides the life of Benedictine monasteries throughout the world. Chapters 33 and 34 deal with property ownership in the monastery. The *Rule* is very clear that no monk is permitted to own anything. Each monk may use only those things that the abbot grants him. At the same time, as much as possible, each monk should have everything he needs, even if it is more or less than what is granted to another monk. Once again, the goal is sufficiency, not excess. No one is to do without what is needed, but no one should have much more than he needs.

The Church continues to maintain its belief in the universal destination of goods. This means that God has given all good things to meet the needs of *all* people, not just a few people or those able to acquire for themselves what they need. The absolute right to private property is limited by the needs of those who lack basic necessities:

> *The universal destination of goods entails obligations on how goods are to be used by their legitimate owners.* Individual persons may not use their resources without considering the effects that this use will have, rather they must act in a way that benefits not only themselves and their family but also the common good. From this there arises the duty on the part of owners not to let the goods in their possession go idle and to channel them to productive activity, even entrusting them to others who are desirous and capable of putting them to use in production. (*Compendium of the Social Doctrine of the Church*, 178, emphasis in original)

That fancy theological language boils down to this: No one has a right to have more than he or she can use. We should share the excess we have with those who need it or who can make use of it.

St. John Chrysostom, the great preacher and Bishop of Constantinople, took it one step further. He criticized even those people who used their excess wealth to equip churches with lavish decorations and vessels instead of giving it to the poor:

> Would you do honor to Christ's body? Neglect him not when naked; do not while here you honor him with silken garments, neglect him perishing without of cold and nakedness. . . .

God has no need at all of golden vessels, but of golden souls.

And these things I say, not forbidding such offerings to be provided; but requiring you, together with them, and before them, to give alms. For he accepts indeed the former, but much more the latter. For in the one the offerer alone is profited, but in the other the receiver also. Here the act seems to be a ground even of ostentation; but there all is mercifulness, and love to man.

For what is the profit, when his table indeed is full of golden cups, but he perishes with hunger? First fill him, being hungered, and then abundantly deck out his table also. Do you make him a cup of gold, while you give him not a cup of cold water? And what is the profit? (*Homilies on Matthew 50*, #4)

The possessions that clutter our homes belong to the poor. By acquiring and keeping much more than we can ever use, we hurt our brothers and sisters who are in need.

All Creation Is Groaning

Finally, clutter has a negative impact on our environment at every point in its life cycle. Making the products that will add to our clutter often involves extracting resources from the earth, for example, through mining or drilling. The pressure to keep costs low increases the risk that these processes will hurt the environment through spills or other accidents or by destroying the habitation of plants and animals. In some places, the land has been stripped of vital nutrients, leading to desertification. Because no food grows in these regions, people are forced to move or starve, increasing tensions and putting pressure on the supplies of food, water, and land in the ever more crowded places to which they move. Industrial production may poison the air and water with by-products. Transporting goods consumes scarce, often nonrenewable fuels, and adds to pollution. Science indicates that the use of these fossil fuels contributes to climate change, with its devastating effects on the planet and the poor. All too often, the prices of the things we buy do not reflect the true costs of their production because they do not include the impact on the environment.

The Church's understanding of the common good means that consumption's effects on the environment and the poor are spiritual concerns as well. Failure to care for the land, air, and water that the Lord has made shows a lack of gratitude for this gift. Since God created each human being in his own image and likeness, we must see God in each of our brothers and sisters in need and extend to them the same love that we would show God. This self-sacrificing love is at the heart of our Christian mission.

So what can I do to place the common good ahead of my clutter and my need to acquire? I can choose to be satisfied with less and grateful for what I have instead of always seeking to buy new things. I can repurpose and reuse what I already have and recycle what can no longer be used. I can slow the pace of the economic treadmill by living more simply, spending time with the people I love rather than spending money on buying more things. When I do need to buy things, I can look past what is most fashionable or what brings the most status. Instead, I can choose where to shop based on things such as whether workers are treated with respect and dignity and whether the merchant is a good citizen of the community. I can pay a bit more for products that are energy efficient, ethically sourced, and environmentally friendly. I can reallocate all the time I spend searching for the best deal to researching my purchases to find those products that best support the common good.

My Journey

I have a problem with food. (No, this isn't suddenly going to turn into a diet book.) I love to cook, and I love to eat. Unfortunately, both can add to my clutter. Because I like to cook, over the years I've collected a lot of utensils and serving ware. Sometimes, I need a specific pan or utensil to make something. And I do love the decorative trays that I use for my annual Christmas party. But eventually, I have to store all of those implements I use only once or twice a year. In other cases, I've upgraded to better quality utensils that are longer lasting and more reliable. Those are reasonable purchases for someone who cooks a lot, but a problem arises when I upgrade but don't replace. It's fine to buy a new nonstick skillet that really doesn't stick. But then I have to get rid of the old one. In too many cases, I've kept both the old and the new, meaning that my storage space is full to bursting.

Then there are the mugs and plastic storage containers. I truly believe that we have enough of each to give everyone on the planet at least one or two! I really need storage containers. I keep leftover food to eat the next day, and I often prepare ingredients ahead of time and need to store them. But if I can't find a matching container and top, what good are they? And while I drink hot beverages occasionally, I rarely have a need for more than ten or twelve mugs at a time (and that assumes that I'm having friends over). It seems that when people don't know what to buy a casual friend as a gift, a mug is the default option. I could get behind a five-year moratorium on giving mugs to anyone. That might give us time to deal with the surplus!

So I already have a kitchen that's packed a bit too tight with cooking utensils and serving ware. This difficulty is compounded by the fact that, by the time I finish cooking, especially on a weeknight, the last thing I want to do is clean up and put everything away neatly. And if I have to spend twenty minutes looking for a container to hold the leftover spaghetti, it's even less likely that everything goes back to where it belongs. So the unwashed dishes and the ingredients left out on the counter just add to the clutter.

Fortunately, the same decluttering process that I used for my clothes will work with kitchen utensils. I need to donate the usable things that I use rarely, if ever. The things used only seasonally need to be stored apart from the items I use daily. (Maybe I can store my Christmas serving ware in the same place as my decorations and my long underwear!) If things are no longer usable or they are incomplete (such as my storage containers without lids), it's time for them be recycled into something usable.

On the eating side, cooking for one person without excessive waste is a real challenge. I have to admit that wasting food triggers my Catholic guilt, especially since Pope Francis regularly reminds me that the food I waste is taken from the poor. But that guilt doesn't help me declutter my pantry and freezer.

One of my problems is that I buy too much. Larger containers usually have lower unit costs. When I buy a gallon of milk, each ounce costs less than if I buy a quart. Of course, that lower cost presumes that I use all of the milk I buy. In other cases, if I buy a larger size or multiple packages, I get a special price. Those purchases can fill my pantry pretty quickly. Because I like to cook, I try a lot of new recipes. A shocking number of those recipes require that I buy ingredients I don't keep in stock. The leftovers end up in the pantry, hidden in the back until I find an appealing new recipe that uses the same ingredients—or until they go bad.

It can be very difficult to cook just one portion, so I tend to cook too much. Most recipes are scaled to four servings and can't be reduced easily. When I cook from scratch, I can't roast a single serving chicken or make just one portion of soup. That means I either have to eat the same thing several days in a row, have friends over for dinner regularly, or freeze part of what I cook. With my refrigerator and freezer full as well, too much food goes bad before I can eat it, adding to my waste.

The best and simplest strategy to address food clutter, and the one I struggle to implement, is to plan my meals before I go grocery shopping. Planning would allow me to decide how to use my leftovers before I start cooking. With enough creative planning, I can even repurpose some leftovers into a whole new dish to avoid eating the same thing over several days. Menu planning would also allow me to make the best use of food I already have. I could choose meals that use up the vegetables in the freezer or the staples in the pantry. Once the meals are planned, I can make a shopping list, double-checking to make sure I'm not buying anything I already have. (In a related question, does anyone need onion powder or whole cloves? I'm asking for a friend.)

To make decluttering the pantry more fun, I some-times play a game with myself. I place three or four items on the kitchen counter and challenge myself to come up with a menu that uses them up within a week. Some of the resulting recipes become favorites; others become funny stories. Pulling these ingredients from the pantry also gives me a reason to rearrange the cabinets, moving older foods to the front so that I can use them before they go bad and taking out items that I'm unlikely to use. The latter items I can donate to a food pantry. The same rear-rangement strategy works for the refrigerator and freezer as well.

Taking my commitment to the common good to heart, I can collaborate with neighbors to share large packages and bulk purchases. We can divide a ten-pound bag of potatoes or each take one package in a "buy one, get one" promotion. Neighborly cooperation is even more helpful in warehouse stores and at farmers' markets that sell by the bushel or crate.

Getting my food purchases under control is a continuing struggle. I'd like to be able to focus on eating seasonally, buying from local producers as much as possible. I'd like to put my money where my mouth is by buying more food produced in ethical ways—with concern for the workers, for the environment, and for the animals involved. Perhaps I could even grow and preserve some of my own food. I already compost as a way to address some of the food waste that I can't conquer. At least the fruit that goes bad ends up in the earth, not the landfill. I'm not yet where I want to be, but conversion is a journey, not a moment, so I keep moving forward.

Signposts for Your Journey

So your decluttering is proceeding well. You've discovered the floor of your closet, and you can actually close the kitchen cabinets. Congratulations! But now you have bags of things that you've decided to give away. What do you do with them?

It's really important to get these things out of your house as quickly as possible. If the bags of goods to be donated stick around for several weeks, they just become more clutter for you to navigate around. And the longer they are in your house, the longer you have to fight the temptation to pull things out. So many times I've put books or clothes into the donation bag only to pull them out a few weeks later, "just for a few days." Before I know it, that sweater is back in the drawer and the book is on my nightstand.

The first step is making sure that everything you plan to give away is usable. Things that are in good condition and still in common use can have a new life. You may want to sell some things at a yard sale, or you can donate them to a thrift store or to an agency that resettles refugees or provides transitional housing for the homeless—or perhaps to a halfway house that helps incarcerated men and women reintegrate into society. The clothes, backpacks, bedding, and toys your children have outgrown might help children moving into foster care who often leave their homes with next to nothing. A soft blanket and a stuffed animal can give them something of their own in a world where everything seems uncertain.

Think about nontraditional places to donate. Libraries and schools may be happy to receive donations of books. Schools and day care centers might be able to use craft supplies or old magazines. Nursing homes may accept DVDs of classic films and old vinyl records. Animal shelters and rescue groups can use old towels and bedding. (Rescued puppies rarely care that the orange flowers on the bedspread clash with their fur!) For larger donations, you may need to call ahead to arrange a pickup or to ensure that staff is available to receive your donation. In some places, scheduling a pickup can take several weeks, so you'll need to plan ahead.

If you don't think something is in good enough condition to keep using, please don't donate it. Charities waste their precious, limited resources sorting trash from useful goods and paying to haul the trash away. Don't undermine your generosity by donating things no one can use, such as stained clothing or incomplete games. People often believe that the poor should be grateful for whatever they receive, but lacking money doesn't mean you lack feelings or dignity. Please respect the people who will receive your donated goods. If you wouldn't use it, why should they? Also, do some research to ensure that your donation will actually go to the intended cause. If you want your donation to go to someone who needs it, don't give it to an organization that sells anything it receives. Some charities use donated goods locally. Others ship things overseas. It's worth an hour or two to check out the charities. Most post their financial reports online, and various watchdog groups provide additional information.

To further connect your decluttering efforts with your faith, look for local faith-based organizations that might make good use of your donations:

- Catholic Charities: Most dioceses have a local Catholic Charities that might be able to use your donations in many ways: for recently resettled refugees, in transitional housing for homeless men and women, or for people reestablishing homes after incarceration.
- Catholic Worker House: A local Catholic Worker house may have a clothes closet accessible to those in need. They may also be able to use furniture or other household goods.
- St. Vincent de Paul Society: Often organized by parish or region, the St. Vincent de Paul Society may receive donations of food, clothing, and household goods that will be shared with those in need.
- The Gabriel Project: This parish-based group helps women facing challenging pregnancies so that they can choose life. It's a great way to recycle clothing for babies and toddlers as well as other baby paraphernalia you no longer need (baby monitors, high chairs, toys, and the like).

For things that are no longer usable, recycling should be the first choice. Many local jurisdictions offer recycling or safe disposal even of large or dangerous items, such as appliances, electronics, and household chemicals. Depending on the item and your community, the recycling might be available through curbside pickup, through a general drop-off point, or at special events. Some communities, and even some retailers, recycle textiles, giving your stained clothes and faded curtains new life as factory rags and insulation.

Thoughts for the Journey

- Am I discarding things I hardly used? If so, why did I buy them in the first place? What need were they intended to fill?
- When I need to make a purchase, do I consider factors other than price and quality? How do I assess the broader impacts of my purchases?
- How do my possessions affect my relationship with my friends? The poor? The earth? God?

Try This

Choose a store that you frequent or a large purchase that you need to make. Research the company or companies involved (the store, manufacturer, etc.) to evaluate the social impact of your purchase. You might want to ask about how each company treats its workers, its charitable involvement in the community, and the ways it does or does not care for the environment. Journal or talk with your accountability partner about what you have learned and how it will affect your behavior as a consumer.

7.

Clutter and Spiritual Discipline

I wish I could say that my decluttering is complete and I'm now enjoying living my well-balanced life in my well-organized home. I wish I could say that all it took was a yearlong focus on each room in turn to change my world. Well, I could say those things, but they wouldn't be true. This wasn't the first time I've undertaken a systematic decluttering. I've decluttered several times, usually in connection with a move or spring-cleaning. But within a year or so, it seems as if I'm back where I started.

The same thing happens in my life of faith. I go on retreat and come back renewed and ready to love God with my whole being (cf. Mt 22:37). Or I truly live Lent in fasting, prayer, and almsgiving and come to Easter prepared to live in the joy of the Resurrection. But somehow, as the days go on, the commitment fades and I'm back to my old ways, fitting prayer in when it's convenient, rushing past those in need, living according to my own priorities instead of according to God's will.

God's Path
Practice Makes Perfect

The gospels tell us the story of Jesus' Transfiguration (cf. Mk 9:2–8). Jesus took Peter, James, and John to the top of a mountain where they saw him in his full glory, conversing with Moses and Elijah. Yet even having seen this miracle, once they came down the mountain, the disciples struggled to understand the nature of Jesus' mission. They did not understand what Jesus had revealed when he declared that "whoever wishes to come after me must deny himself, take up his cross, and follow me" (Mt 16:24). Though encouraged and inspired by what took place on the mountaintop, the disciples found it hard to maintain their enthusiasm once the challenges of "real life" again held sway. They were prepared to travel with Jesus as he preached and healed and worked wondrous signs, but rejection and death were more than they'd bargained for. Of course keeping my home tidy and well organized isn't a matter of life and death, but I do struggle to stay focused and committed when life gets hectic (as it always does). I want the result but not the work that achieving it will require.

Several years ago, I decided that I was going to start running; nothing major, just a few 5K races for causes that mean a lot to me. So I did my somewhat sporadic training and managed to survive a few races though my times were very slow. Then I decided that I needed to do more, to push myself harder. So I signed up for a half marathon. I did have the good sense to give myself more than a year to prepare. I built a training plan that let me increase distance and speed slowly. Over the course of several months, I went from races of five kilometers to eight kilometers to ten kilometers to ten miles. But those races were the smallest part of my efforts. They were just chances to run with lots of other people on new courses with accurate timing to tell me how fast I was running (spoiler alert: not very).

The real work came between the races. Several days a week, I ran shorter distances, working on pace and technique. On off days, I did cross training to improve my strength and cardiovascular fitness. One day a week, I would go for a long run, increasing the distance every few weeks. By the time my half-marathon rolled around, I knew I could cover the 13.1 miles necessary because I had done it several times in training. Finishing that race while meeting my goal time (thirteen-minute miles, in case you were wondering) was the capstone, but the real work was done in the months before. Unfortunately, I stopped running seriously about a year later. So if I want to start running long races again, I'll have to go back to the beginning and rebuild. But at least I know how to do it.

I tell this story because it's an analogy for both decluttering and my life of faith. The big decluttering or the amazing silent retreat, like the half marathon, is a "mountaintop" moment like the Transfiguration. I plan for each and work hard to get there. But while it's great to stand on the mountaintop basking in my success, I need to do more to make the change last when it's not all blinding sunlight and chatting prophets. Now, maybe I don't have to run eight miles every Saturday or take everything out of all my closets or be silent for five days—but I do need to maintain my momentum. Once I let inertia set in, it takes over quickly. For example, when I get out of the habit of daily prayer or weekly Mass or trying to discern God's will, it becomes progressively easier to let my religious practice slide and to make decisions selfishly, with no concern for others. So although I stopped doing long runs, I might need to keep up the pace and technique runs or the cross training. Once the decluttering is complete, I still need to be careful about what comes into my house and how I manage my possessions and my schedule. After the retreat, after Easter, I need to continue to make time for God every day, discerning his will to set my path.

Lifelong Learning

I find it particularly telling that the words *disciple* and *discipline* have the same root, a Latin word meaning "pupil," one who learns. Being a disciple is about learning how to live like Jesus. It requires discipline. This discipline isn't sitting in the timeout chair thinking about what I've done. This discipline is the daily taming of selfish desires, the daily taking up of my cross to follow Jesus more closely. In the early Church, you didn't become a Christian by just asking or by filling out forms or by taking a class in Church teaching. People who wanted to be baptized spent a period of time (sometimes years) learning how to live like a Christian under the guidance of an established member of the community. This period before baptism, called the catechumenate, was a time of apprenticeship, of learning by doing. After all, knowledge, no matter how valuable, isn't enough. Action is necessary. I can read any number of volumes on homekeeping and organizing, but that doesn't matter unless I put what I learn into practice. I can read any number of books about theology, but that does not make me a good Christian.

Learning by doing will take time and effort—and failure. Let me give you an example. I came to the art of cooking rather late—in my thirties, actually. Even as a child, I wanted to learn to cook. I just wasn't any good at it. (Seriously—ask my family about the cookie recipe that they wanted to sell to the Department of Transportation to use for filling potholes). When I decided to learn to cook, I bought cookbooks, watched cooking shows, and even cooked with friends who are skilled. But ultimately, watching wasn't enough. I had to start cooking, day in and day out. It didn't always go well. It still doesn't. (I have the worst time getting things to just the right state of done.) But as I continued to practice, I got better. Eventually, I could even develop my own recipes for dishes that people wanted to eat! In time, I was able to teach other people some of the things I had learned, even while I kept learning myself.

Keeping clutter at bay will require the same sort of effort. I have to keep practicing. Every time I declutter, my process is a bit more efficient and it goes more smoothly. Every time I declutter, I find it a bit easier to let go of items that I once thought were essential. Every time I declutter, I detach a bit more from my possessions. It may be slow (like my running), but it's progress. Even though I'm really committed to this effort, I know that I'll have setbacks. There will be weeks (months?) when I won't be able to open a cabinet without things falling out. There will be days when I buy things that I know I don't need. I'm an imperfect person in the process of being perfected. I know that I will fail sometimes. It's my response to those failures that matters. I can learn from my mistakes and try to do better in the future, or I can abandon my effort and go back to accumulating clutter with renewed vigor.

The way I grow in faith parallels my decluttering effort. Long before I ever read a theology book or took a religion class, I learned how to be a person of faith by watching my grandmother pray, by going to Mass every Sunday with my parents, and by following the examples of my family members and teachers. When I failed, they corrected me gently and I learned—slowly. The Church offers many opportunities to help me develop and maintain the discipline I need to be a good disciple. The Sunday obligation to attend Mass and the call to pray each day are constant reminders to keep God at the center of my life and to seek his will in everything that I do. When I fail, as I always do, the Sacrament of Penance celebrates God's mercy and forgiveness. In this sacrament, God forgives my sins and his grace strengthens me to follow his will more closely in the future. With this gift of grace and my renewed purpose, I hope as time goes on, I get better and better at following God's will.

Going Against the Trend

Defeating clutter and living a Christian life both require living by values that are very different from those most lauded in our culture. Defeating clutter means changing our relationship with material things, moving from possessiveness to detachment. In an economy based on continual purchasing where the newest and biggest is best, declining to shop and being content with what we have are radical acts. We are bombarded with enticements to buy more, consume more, accumulate more. On a daily basis, we encounter advertising in the newspaper, on television, through e-mail, and even on our phones! At times, we are even told that buying more is the selfless, patriotic thing to do since it supports the economy!

Rejecting these enticements requires commitment and a firm sense of purpose. It may also mean that we have to do things differently. For example, I love to give gifts. Christmas is my favorite holiday. I spend the entire year looking for the right things to give the people I love. There's a reason that my friends call me "Elf." But most people on my gift list have everything they need. So I've had to find ways to reconcile my love for giving gifts with my desire to not add to the clutter. I've come up with a few strategies that seem to work.

Sometimes, I'm able to give a gift that replaces an item that has ended its useful life. The old item goes to recycling and clutter is held at bay. Another strategy is to give an experience of some sort—a tour, a class, or tickets to an event. These gifts don't add to the clutter because there's always room for more memories. Some people love having donations made in their names, but I'm always careful to give to causes that are meaningful to them. I can give consumable gifts if I know a person's tastes well. In some cases, I've agreed with friends to stop exchanging gifts that we don't need. Instead, we use that money to do something together, giving the gift of time and attention. I've had to change my common practice and go against the cultural norm to stay faithful to my desire to step off the consumption train.

On a more fundamental level, defeating clutter requires that I reject the value system so prevalent in society today. Too often, people are judged by their wealth and influence, as if the ability to buy beautiful things is evidence of their goodness and intelligence. But the same Christian faith that has led me to try to break my attachment to my material possessions reminds me that my worth and the worth of other people depends not on what we own but on the fact that we are children of God, made in his image and likeness. In fact, the simpler and more childlike we are, the closer we are to God: "Amen, I say to you, unless you turn and become like children, you will not enter the kingdom of heaven. Whoever humbles himself like this child is the greatest in the kingdom of heaven" (Mt 18:3–4).

Choosing to live an authentic Christian life is a radical step. Living for God, pouring your life out for others, and reaching out to those on the margins is the opposite of how today's society judges success. Those who perform good deeds may become the occasional "overnight sensation," but most of the people who spend their lives helping others do so well outside the spotlight. Instead, people are held up as role models because they achieve wealth and fame and live in comfort or even luxury. Social pressure encourages us to imitate their example (and to buy the products they promote). But that's not the way of faith, the way of Christ. Instead, Jesus said that "everyone who exalts himself will be humbled, but the one who humbles himself will be exalted" (Lk 14:11). And he had difficult words for those who relied on their worldly wealth: "Woe to you who are rich, for you have received your consolation" (Lk 6:24). He even said that "it is easier for a camel to pass through the eye of a needle than for one who is rich to enter the kingdom of God" (Mt 19:24).

These passages don't mean that material goods are bad. Remember, Jesus used material things (bread, wine, fish, and mud) to perform his miracles. But they do warn us that relying on these material goods for safety, for fulfillment, and for joy is a dead-end path. We can't pass through a tight door carrying lots of bags. Only when we drop what we are carrying can we enter with ease.

The Never-Ending Story

One of the most frustrating things about both decluttering and the spiritual life is the fact that they are never done. Housekeeping in general is a thankless, unending task. No matter how hard we work, there will always be more to do. We can finish all the laundry and scrub all the floors, but in a matter of days, the hampers will be filled again and the floors will be tracked with mud. We'll be right back where we started. When I don't keep up with my tidying, the clutter returns all too quickly. Well-ordered spaces descend into chaos and it becomes hard to find things that I need. I can never say, "Enough! I'm done!" and just rest.

In the same way, the decision to follow Christ is not a one-time thing. Jesus told us that we would have to decide each day to take up our crosses and follow him. We never get to say, "Well, that's enough being Christian for this week. I'm done." Living an authentic Christian life isn't something we can drop in on occasionally. It's not enough to go to church on Christmas and Easter and remember to avoid eating meat on Fridays during Lent. All of those things are good, but they're not really enough to support our Christian living.

One of the hallmarks of the modern world is that the pace of life has increased. Everything seems faster, because it is. Instead of taking months or even years to send letters or travel via messengers and ships, we can communicate with people around the world in a matter of seconds. Instead of patiently tending crops while sun, rain, and time help them grow and ripen, our work is expected "stat" or "ASAP," or we hear, "I needed it yesterday." Everything seems to move with great urgency. So it's really no wonder that we tend to move from crisis to crisis in our spiritual and our domestic lives. We go from manic tidying so that we can welcome guests or celebrate Christmas to leaving the dishes in the dishwasher for a week because we haven't run out of cereal bowls yet. We beg God to hear us when we face illness, the death of a loved one, or fears for a child and then seemingly forget that God exists once the crisis has passed—or hold God responsible for a negative outcome.

A life marked by spiritual discipline can help to break this cycle. I find the example of John the Baptist to be very helpful. He serves as the ultimate example of simple living. He doesn't seem to have had a home. His clothes were of the simplest sort, garments of camels' hair and a leather belt. Even his food (locusts and wild honey) was what he could scavenge. No room for clutter there! We know him as the one who prepared the way for Jesus, and how he did that can help shed some light on our spiritual efforts to make room for God. As Isaiah prophesied centuries before John and Jesus lived, John prepared the way by leveling the hills and filling the valleys. He made the way to Jesus easier to traverse, not lurching from peak to valley but following a level path. And as Luke tells us, he did this by admonishing people to be satisfied with what they had and to share with those in need (cf. Lk 3:10–14). Even today, this same advice can guide us to a more balanced, spirit-filled, organized life. We need to develop the spiritual discipline that allows us to be satisfied with our possessions, grateful to the God who provided them, and generous in sharing them with those who are in need. By disciplining our wills, we will find an easier path to the One whose disciples we are privileged to be.

My Journey

I really want this declutter to last. While I know that I won't be perfect, I'd at least like to avoid ending up back where I started. I don't want to revert to a situation that will take days or even weeks to restore to order. To accomplish my goal, I need to make dealing with clutter part of my routine. To many people, *routine* is a dirty word. But routines give me structure and, ultimately, freedom. With a routine, certain activities become second nature. I don't waste time wondering what I need to do since I know what I have to do each day. A routine creates a rhythm that adds to the serenity and order in my life. Of course, there are times when I disrupt my routine. But having a basic routine in place keeps me on the right track.

If you've made it to chapter 7, you've noticed that I like order and planning. So it probably won't surprise you that I have daily and weekly routines. The best part of my daily routines is that they don't take long. I can work them in as easily as brushing my teeth and washing my face. Plus, they help me start and end my days on the right note. Since I'm no longer scrolling through my news feed every morning before I get out of bed because I started keeping my phone across the room, I've found ten extra minutes to do some quick tidying. That means I have time to make my bed, put away the dishes left in the drying rack over-night, pack my lunch, and gather anything I need to take to work. I even have time to put the recyclables into their proper bin and toss any food scraps into the compost pile. All that, and I can still walk the dog and get to work on time.

The night routine is a bit more challenging for me since I have a tendency to keep working or checking my Twitter feed or watching television until I'm just about falling over. That's bad for my sense of order and bad for my sleep. Numerous studies have shown that people sleep better when they disconnect from electronics at least fifteen to thirty minutes before they go to sleep. By doing that, I can get two benefits at once! I can get a more restful night's sleep and wake up to a tidy house. So what do I do in the thirty minutes before bed? I make sure that any dishes in the sink are washed and in the rack to dry over-night and that the sink is clean. If I do the dishes right after dinner like I should, they'll be ready to put away. Any-thing I brought out during the evening (reference books, crafting supplies, etc.) goes back to where it belongs. I gather up and wash the glasses and bowls from my late night snack. I put the newspaper, junk mail, and any magazines I've finished reading on the stack to recycle in the morning. I hang up any clothes left on the chair in my bedroom. Finally, I decide what I'm going to wear to work the next day and get it out so that I don't have to fumble in my closet or drawers before my eyes are fully open.

These little routines may not seem like much, but I wake up more rested and to a greater sense of order. I'm calm and ready to pray Morning Prayer when I get on the subway. When I finish work and get on the subway to go home, I pray Evening Prayer to mark the transition in my day. I come home to a tidy house (and a barking dog). Once I walk the barking dog, I'm ready to light a candle, start dinner (using my weekly menu plan), and embrace whatever the evening holds, be it chores, reading, some needlework, or a good hockey game on television. Of course, there are days when the routine goes out the window. I oversleep, and it's all I can do to get dressed and walk the dog before I dash to work, a granola bar in my hand. (Trust me, not walking the dog is not an option.) On the other side, I may get home late from an event or become engrossed in that hockey game until I'm practically asleep in my chair. But that's the great thing about a routine. If you miss it one day, you pick it up the next and you're back on schedule. Maybe the routine takes a few minutes more that next day, but it won't be overwhelming.

My weekly routine is actually kind of fun. By the time my workweek comes to an end, I'm tired, mentally and physically. But I still want to be able to enjoy my weekend and not worry about the condition of my house. So I created the Friday tidy (say it out loud—it almost rhymes!). After I get home from work (and walk the dog), I change clothes and put on some loud music with a great beat (if you prefer classical music, Mahler was made for this!). As I sing and dance along with the music, I do a quick once-over of the main rooms of the house (bathroom, master bedroom, living room, and kitchen). I'll give the bathroom fixtures a quick clean and set out fresh towels. I make sure that my morning routine really left my bedroom tidy. If there are still clothes sitting out, I put them away or in the hamper. If I have time, I may even run a quick dust rag over the dresser. Since the living room should still be tidy because of my morning and evening routine, I just make sure everything is in its place and give it a quick sweep. (That dog I keep walking will carry leaves in on her paws.) In the kitchen, I make sure the sink and dish rack are empty and everything that should be in the cabinets is in place. If I'm feeling industrious, I may run a damp mop over the floor. I know that this sounds like a lot, but I'm not doing any deep cleaning. I'm just doing a quick catch-up from the week. It rarely takes me even a full hour. Once the Friday tidy is done, I pop dinner in the oven and hit the shower. I'm ready for a restful evening watching television or reading and then a great weekend. Of course, sometimes I'm out on Friday evening. In that case, I can move the routine to Thursday or even skip it for a week. But I get back into rhythm as quickly as possible.

Even though I work daily to keep the clutter at bay, it will do its best to reappear. I'll pick up some new books but not donate any old ones. I'll buy some new clothes. I'll have more paperwork that needs to be filed. I use spring and fall cleaning to keep ahead of the game. If I do my spring cleaning after I file my taxes, I know what paperwork I need to keep and what I can shred. (As a bonus, you can often find free bulk shredding events around this time of year. I told you in the preface that I'm cheap.) Switching to my spring and summer clothes is a great time to donate the clothes I don't wear or that no longer fit. Reducing the clutter first makes deep spring-cleaning that much easier. In the fall, I reverse things as I get my winter clothes out of storage and put away outdoor furniture and sports equipment. Anything that isn't used doesn't go into storage. My summer beach books get donated. Fall cleaning sets the stage for my holiday decorating and entertaining.

Signposts for Your Journey

Now you must be thinking, "Well, isn't that nice for her? She has a small house and no kids. Let's see her do that in my house while trying to get the kids to school." Dealing with decluttering as a family certainly adds to the complexity, but there's no reason that keeping things tidy can't be a family project. Kids thrive on routine. They like the certainty of knowing what comes next. Think about the following nighttime routine: bathe, brush teeth, put away toys, put clothes in the hamper, set out clothes for the morning, say bedtime prayers with Mommy and Daddy, read story together. The daily rhythm lets kids know that it's time to settle down to sleep.

Even preschool children can learn to put their toys back in the toy chest before bed and to put their dirty clothes into a laundry bag. Many kids enjoy helping with household tasks because it makes them feel grown-up. As children age, they should become more responsible for keeping their own rooms tidy and they should help with family chores. (If you can drive a car, you can run a washing machine.) Every family member can help with emptying the dishwasher, taking out trash and recycling, and tidying the family room and the bathrooms. The results may not be perfect, but this is one time when it's important to praise sincere effort. Maybe you wouldn't have put Mr.

Teddy Bear into the dishwasher because he was dirty, but the thought wasn't far off.

Creating a family tidying routine will help to build good habits for the future. A tidying routine can be fun. Try setting a timer for fifteen or twenty minutes and see who can tidy the most before the buzzer rings. Friday tidy is a lot more fun if it ends with family movie and pizza night. (Maybe whoever tidied the most can pick the movie.)

Maybe you aren't ready to create a routine. That doesn't mean you can't do anything. Pick three or four places in your house where clutter tends to gather. Mine are the mail table, the chair in my bedroom, the box of filing, and the bag I carry to work. Focus on those places only, and try your best to keep them clutter free. Pick one day each week as a target and tell yourself, "On Sunday, the mail table will be empty" or "On Tuesday, there will be no filing in the box." When you see the progress you can make on this small scale, it will be easier to expand your efforts. Success will build confidence. As the clutter in your home decreases, you'll become more careful about bringing unnecessary items into the house. When you do get new things, you'll be more ready to move old possessions out to keep balance. There will be stumbles, but you can always try again.

Thoughts for the Journey

- What spiritual experience have I had that I could describe as a mountaintop experience? How long was I able to hold on to the inspiration I felt after that experience?
- Who taught me how to live as a Christian? Who is teaching me now? Whom am I teaching?
- What steps can I take this week to break the cycle of moving from crisis to crisis?

Try This

Write down your daily or weekly routine, and post it in a place where you can see it every day (perhaps on the back of your bedroom door or inside a kitchen cabinet). Follow the routine carefully for a month and then reexamine the routine, either alone or with your accountability partner, to see how you can modify the routine to make it easy to maintain and more effective.

Conclusion

This book has been a journey moving toward two goals: a clutter-free house and a closer relationship with God. We've looked at how God uses the material goods of the world to show his love for us and how those same goods help us to hold on to memories of the people and experiences that have shaped our lives. On the shadow side, we explored how sin can mar our relationship with our possessions and keep us from loving God with all our hearts. So then we turned to the ways that practicing penance can help us change our hearts so that our love of God and neighbor takes precedence. Our communication with God in prayer can guide and sustain us in his will, to receive his gifts with gratitude and share them generously. We considered how the things we own can have an impact on the poor and the environment—and how that impact affects our relationship with God. Finally, we looked at how spiritual discipline can help us maintain both the clutter-free homes we've created and the faith-filled lives we desire. Through it all, I've shared with you my own decluttering journey, with all of its joys and hopes, griefs and anxieties. And I've offered encouragement to you as you embark on your journey.

As you've dealt with your own clutter, you may have encountered both challenges and gifts. Some of the memories you unearthed may have been painful. Seeing a letter written by a loved one now gone can make the grief feel fresh again. Sorting through unnecessary purchases may arouse feelings of guilt and failure, and you may simply feel overwhelmed. But God is waiting for you and for me in these challenges, offering comfort in our grief, forgiveness for our failures, hope in place of guilt, and courage to face the sometimes daunting tasks ahead. At the same time, dealing with clutter may unearth more than an unexpired gift card from Aunt Emma. Sorting through our possessions can make us more aware of the bountiful gifts God has shared with us. As we sort through family heirlooms and old Christmas gifts, we are reminded of the love that surrounds us. The process itself can help us focus on our priorities, use our time well, and practice patience.

Throughout this book, I've talked about the similarities between decluttering and the spiritual life. Now, in these final pages, I have to talk about the very important way that they differ. Dealing with clutter and getting organized is all about having a place for everything. If you have too much stuff, it overflows the space available and becomes clutter. When you limit your possessions and have a proper place for every item, you know what you have and where to find it. Life is more predictable and ordered. The order provides a certainty that is very comforting.

When I was in high school, I provided in-home day care for a few families. In those long days, I learned that every nanny faces three great challenges: getting kids to eat, getting kids down for their naps, and, getting the toys put away before the mom gets home. (It has not escaped me that we grow out of the first two as we grow older. At my age, lunch that someone else cooked and a nap sound like a treat!) Kids have to be taught to put their things away, but when those are in place, they take a certain pride in knowing exactly where Mr. Teddy Bear is (and that he survived his visit to the dishwasher). From a very young age, we like the reassurance and comfort that order provides—even as we take pleasure in occasionally causing chaos.

But this need to put objects in their proper place, to compartmentalize things, is where decluttering and spirituality part company. We can't compartmentalize God. Our relationship with him needs to enter every aspect of our lives—every hope, dream, and fear, every relationship and every struggle, every success and every failure. Everything we say and do must carry us further along the path so that "God may be all in all" (1 Cor 15:28).

Our existence finds its purpose and meaning not in the possessions neatly stored in labeled cabinets but in living as God's children, free from slavery to sin and death, free from attachments to the possessions that weigh us down. At the beginning of this book, I asked if God cared about the clutter in our homes. The simple answer is that God cares about everything that affects us. Our relationship with God isn't something that matters only when we are in church or praying or if we are called to ministry. No matter what we do, God plays a role. We can't separate our lives of faith from our "real lives." We each have one life. As St. Paul wrote to the Romans, "whether we live or die, we are the Lord's" (Rom 14:8).

So where do we go from here? Our decluttering journey will certainly continue. It's not like the temptation to buy things we don't need will suddenly disappear. Opportunities to overindulge will continue to surround us. We will need material goods to survive, so we will need to make purchases. How can we carry on with the normal activities of life without ending up buried in clutter once again?

I hope that the lessons of this decluttering will stay with us. We will receive items gratefully and care for them well, as good stewards. We will treasure the memories that give meaning to life. More aware of the sinful tendencies that tempt us to an unhealthy relationship with possessions, we can combat them with the help of spiritual discipline strengthened by prayer. In making purchases and in deciding what to keep, we can consider how those decisions might affect the poor and the environment. What we learn through the process of decluttering is how to be more intentional about what we buy and how we use the things we own. We don't hide away from the material world; we engage it with renewed focus, with our mind on God's plan.

Decluttering has shown us that we cannot fill the holes in our hearts and in our spirits by acquiring more things. At best, the things we accumulate are only a temporary fix. Eventually, their novelty and utility will fade and we will feel empty once again. All the clutter in the world cannot make us feel whole. Only God can satisfy the needs of our hearts and our spirits. When we begin with gratitude to God and reliance on his provident care, the hole closes, filled with God's presence. Still trying to make room for God? Look inside your heart. He's already there, waiting.

Thoughts for the Journey

- As you've worked your way through this book and through your decluttering, what did you learn about your relationship with God and with your possessions?
- Where did you find unexpected room for more love of God and your neighbor?
- What challenges still remain for you to face?

Try This

After six months, look back at some of the reflection questions or "Try This" exercises in this book to see how far you've come and to check your progress moving forward. Journal or talk with your accountability partner to identify areas that need more work.

Acknowledgments

A constant theme in this book is the importance of gratitude. So it seems appropriate that I begin by saying thank you:

To Lisa Hendey, who first approached me about writing this book and who offered constant encouragement and prayerful support;

To Tom Grady, who suggested me as a possible author for a book like this and whose love for the Church and kindness for his friends has overwhelmed me time and again;

To Eileen Ponder, who edited this book and offered support and advice when I needed it the most, with a little assistance from Isaac Asimov;

To James Rogers and Linda Hunt, my supervisors at the USCCB, who support my writing and who are the very best bosses I could ever hope to have;

To my family, my mother Katherine and my sisters, Kathy and Carol Ann, who love me through it all and who allowed me to test out some decluttering theories on them, and to Hershey, who never seemed to mind when I worked out pieces of chapters while we walked;

To Erica Leighty Blanton, who got me through the last bout of writer's block with a discussion of her work as an organizer and who has given me the gift of her friendship for years;

To Jerry Baumbach, a brilliant catechist and an even better friend;

To Cherie Sprosty and Fred Applegate, who got me thinking about spiritual hoarding;

To the many friends who offered encouragement when I was sure I would never finish this book, especially Noreen Dempsey (my unofficial agent), Vicki Carter and Larry Moran, Nancy McAtee and John St. Clair, Elisabeth Nelson, Lisa LeBlanc, Andrea Proulx Buinicki, Susan Grunder, Jan Stefanow, Colin O'Brien, and the Picketts (Rae, Steve, my godson Henry, and Noah); and

To Christopher Federanich, whose love and support make every day better. I'm so grateful to have you in my life. I love you.

Mary Elizabeth Sperry has worked for the United States Conference of Catholic Bishops since 1994, and serves as associate director for USCCB permissions and NAB utilization.

The author of five books, Sperry's articles have appeared in publications including *Give Us This Day*, *Liguorian*, *Emmanuel*, and *Today's Parish Minister*. She speaks about the Bible and a variety of spiritual topics in dioceses and parishes throughout the United States and has been interviewed on National Public Radio, EWTN Radio, CBS Radio, Relevant Radio, and SiriusXM. Sperry earned a master's degree in liturgical studies from Catholic University of America and a master's degree in political science from the University of California, Los Angeles. She has bachelor's degrees in international politics, Russian, and economics.

She lives in the Washington, DC, area.

AVE

AVE MARIA PRESS

Founded in 1865, Ave Maria Press,
a ministry of the Congregation of
Holy Cross, is a Catholic publishing
company that serves the spiritual and
formative needs of the Church and its
schools, institutions, and ministers;
Christian individuals and families; and
others seeking spiritual nourishment.

For a complete listing of titles from

Ave Maria Press

Sorin Books

Forest of Peace

Christian Classics

visit www.avemariapress.com

AVE | AVE MARIA PRESS
    | Notre Dame, IN
A Ministry of the United States Province of Holy Cross